W9-BWN-583

The Handbook for Reading the Yearly Astrological Calendar

CELESTIAL NAVIGATION FOR SEEKERS OF THE HEAVENS

 Published by RealityIs Books, an imprint of RealityIsBooks.com, Inc., Palatine, IL 60074. Email: publish@RealityIsBooks.com.

Cover photo by fotografiker. Author photo by Catherine Michalski.

First printing 2008
EAN 978-0-9817137-1-7, ISBN 0-9817137-1-8

The Handbook for Reading the Yearly Astrological Calendar

CELESTIAL NAVIGATION FOR SEEKERS OF THE HEAVENS

Anold Lane

TABLE OF CONTENTS

INTRODUCTION

The information contained in this handbook is derived from astrology classes I have taught over several decades. I gave my students a copy of Jim Maynard's *Celestial Guide*®, a yearly astrological calendar, which will be the one referenced throughout this handbook. I showed them how to use it as a tool to move beyond a basic understanding of their natal (birth) charts to a deeper understanding of astrology.

You are holding a handbook to the yearly astrological calendar that will teach you how to interpret the calendar and how to use it for your greatest benefit. You will also learn simple and easily accessible methods for gaining a better understanding of your natal chart and how to use that understanding to make more informed day-to-day choices and better long-term decisions.

This information, published here for the first time, differs in certain respects from other interpretations of astrology. I have reinterpreted some basic astrological concepts to align them with our current understanding of human psychology and spirituality. I have also changed astrological terminology that I consider archaic to terms that better reflect their modern meanings.

The handbook begins with an overview of the *Celestial Guide*®, an explanation of its symbols and how to read and interpret them. Chapter Two discusses the Lunar Cycle, including its important Void of Course phase, and explains how to use each of its phases to your greatest advantage. Chapter Three describes the influences of the planets, explains their symbolism, and their connection to the chakra system. Chapter Four gives the meaning of each sign and describes its liabilities and assets. The significance of houses and how to use the calendar to locate the houses of the New and Full Moon cycles in your natal chart are explored in Chapter Five. The planets in aspect to one another and how to work with these combinations are explained in Chapter Six. Chapters Seven and Eight offer New and Full Moon affirmations that invoke the qualities of the signs, thereby strengthening the opportunities available to you during those times. Chapters Nine and Ten give keywords for each planet and sign that can be used for both the calendar and your natal chart.

As a seeker of the heavens, you are about to embark on a journey that has the potential of a lifetime of learning and growth. Whenever you look to the night sky, remind yourself of the immensity of the celestial realm in which you are an active participant, and gratefully witness its splendor.

Chapter 1

OVERVIEW OF THE *CELESTIAL GUIDE®*

You may have had an astrologer create and interpret a natal chart for you. You have purchased an astrological calendar. Looking at the astrological symbols listed on any given date, you may be wondering how to interpret them, and how they relate to your natal chart. You are holding a tour book that will take you step-by-step through the *Celestial Guide®* and show you how to apply the information given in the calendar to your natal chart and personal circumstances. Gaining an understanding of this material will allow you to derive greater benefit from the knowledge contained in the astrological calendar and your natal chart and, as a result, to live life more consciously day by day.

As you learn to use the calendar, I suggest that you make notes on each day's date about the astrological "weather." Making notes of your experience, combined with what you are reading in the astrological calendar, will engage your left and right brains. The grounding of your experience and the information of your study will be brought together, helping you remember the qualities of the planets and signs. Comprehension will be increased and understanding will come alive for you.

Begin your journey by opening the *Celestial Guide®* to the "Planetary Motions" chart (usually found on page 2). You will notice a circle divided into 12 sections like the spokes of a wheel with the sun at its center. A glyph (symbol) representing each of the 12 signs of the zodiac is drawn just inside of each section, called a house. The signs go counter-clockwise around the circle. The circle represents the "tropical" wheel of the zodiac with Aries positioned at 9 o'clock as the first sign of spring.

This wheel is called the "tropical" or "natural" zodiac because the sun is right over the Tropic of Cancer at the summer solstice and over the Tropic of Capricorn at the winter solstice. Every 30 days the sun travels around the wheel through each sign until it comes back to its spring equinox position. The first day of spring marks the beginning of the tropical zodiac every year on or about March 21st.[1]

Throughout the calendar year, the planets move within the circle. The Planetary Motions chart tells you what signs the planets are in during any given year and how fast they move through the zodiac (Figure 1).

The faster moving planets are closest to the center of the circle, where the Sun is located. The Moon is really a satellite and the Sun is a star. But for simplicity, all of them are called planets, which is from the Greek word meaning "wanderer."

Figure 1

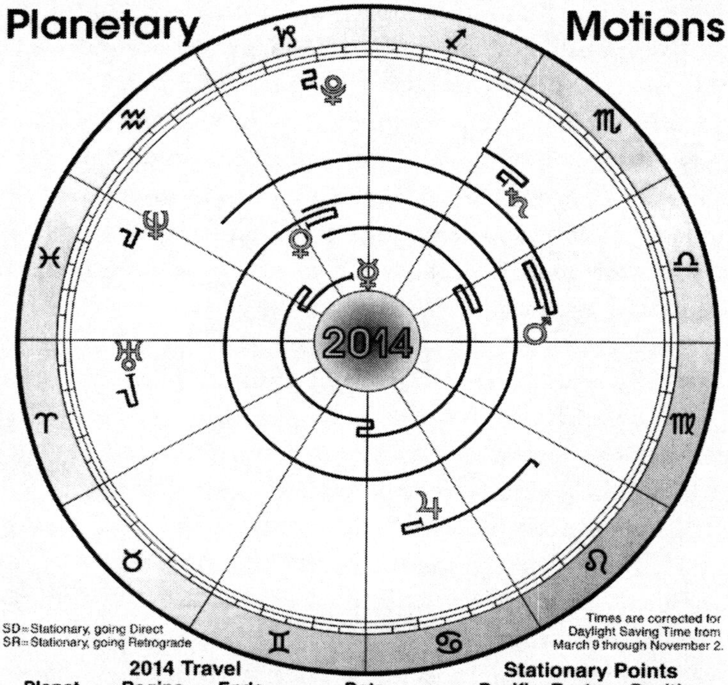

Planetary Motions

2014

SD=Stationary, going Direct
SR=Stationary, going Retrograde

Times are corrected for Daylight Saving Time from March 9 through November 2.

	2014 Travel			Stationary Points			
Planet	Begins	Ends		Date	Pacific	Eastern	Position
Mercury ☿	12♑53	22♑52	SR	February 6	1:43p	4:43p	3♓20
			SD	February 28	6:00a	9:00a	18♒10
			SR	June 7	4:57a	7:57a	3♋10
			SD	July 1	5:50a	8:50a	24♊23
			SR	October 4	10:02a	1:02p	2♏19
			SD	October 25	12:17p	3:17p	16♎46
Venus ♀	26♑41℞	26♑06	SD	January 31	12:49p	3:49p	13♑33
Mars ♂	11♎52	20♒40	SR	March 1	8:24a	11:24a	27♎32
			SD	May 19	6:31p	9:31p	9♎02
Jupiter ♃	16♋03℞	21♌48℞	SD	March 6	2:42a	5:42a	10♋26
			SR	December 8	12:41p	3:41p	22♌38
Saturn ♄	20♏24	0♐49	SR	March 2	8:19a	11:19a	23♏19
			SD	July 20	1:36p	4:36p	16♏39
Uranus ♅	8♈41	12♈36	SR	July 21	7:53p	10:53p	16♈30
			SD	December 21	2:45p	5:45p	12♈34
Neptune ♆	3♓15	5♓23	SR	June 9	12:51p	3:51p	7♓36
			SD	Nov. 15/16	11:06p	2:06a	4♓48
Pluto ♇	11♑16	13♑09	SR	April 14	4:44p	7:44p	13♑35
			SD	September 22	5:34p	8:34p	11♑00

Each planet's motion for the whole year is shown within the circle in this chart. As you look out further from the center of the circle, the arcs showing the planets' orbits around the Sun become shorter. The arcs showing their motion become shorter because the outer planets take longer to orbit around the Sun.

Notice that the outer planets, Uranus, Neptune and Pluto, move a shorter distance in a year than the inner planets. Find the symbol for Pluto. Notice how far it moves in a year. The arc representing Pluto is about a quarter of an inch. Pluto takes 248 years to orbit around the Sun. Compare its motion to Mercury, which goes a little more than once around the Sun in a year.

The closest planetary glyph to the Sun is for the planet Mercury. Because it is the fastest moving planet in the solar system, except for the Moon, Mercury circles further around the sun than the other planets. It is called the messenger planet and is associated with quicksilver. You notice that the arc stops several times and reverses direction clockwise for a short time, again stopping and then moving forward, in what is called direct motion. An arc going backwards in a clockwise motion around the circle depicts a planet's retrograde motion. Direct motion means that the planet is going forward through the zodiac in a counterclockwise direction.

Retrograde is when a planet appears to go backwards in clockwise motion through the natural order of the zodiacal signs. The planets do not stop and change directions. Retrograde motion is an optical illusion, but it does affect us. All planets except the Sun and Moon go retrograde. The most important retrograde cycle to follow is the dates and times for Mercury's retrograde cycle, both beginning and ending times and dates. In the chart below the wheel of planetary motions, the letters SD and SR indicate when each planet goes stationary then direct, and stationary then retrograde.

The Chart of Planetary Motions for each calendar year not only shows you the order of the planets outward from the Sun, but also shows you what signs the planets are going to be in during any particular year. Mercury moves through all the signs in a year. The next planet out away from the center is the female symbol for Venus, which does not move quite as far through the signs around the circle. The male symbol for Mars is next, orbiting slightly more than half way around the circle of the zodiacal signs each year. The next planet out, Jupiter, moves about 30° through the wheel in a year, usually traveling only through two signs. The arc for Saturn, the next planet out, is shorter yet. It changes signs about every 2½ years.

Now we get to the invisible planets. Uranus takes 84 years to go around the zodiac and remains in a sign for about seven years. Neptune takes 165 years to orbit through the zodiac. Pluto, the planet farthest from the center with the shortest arc, takes 248 years to go around the zodiac.

Next look at the page that gives time zone changes. It takes two hours for a shift from one sign to the next to take place over any particular time zone. The 12 signs repeat themselves every 24 hours. In other words, if you were to go outside and see 0° Aries rising on the eastern horizon, and then wait two hours, the next sign, Taurus, would be rising. Every two hours the rising sign for each time zone changes on the eastern horizon. Each day this pattern repeats itself for every time zone because the Earth is spinning on its axis like a top. It takes 24 hours for it to rotate back to the same place.

The stars and constellations are not moving around the earth; the earth is rotating around like a sphere spinning. No wonder the ancients thought the sun was a chariot traveling across the sky. They did not realize it was the Earth's rotation that causes the Sun to appear to be moving across the sky from east to west.

The "Eclipses" page gives the place and time of four eclipses that will occur during the year. If there is a solar eclipse first, then a lunar eclipse follows two weeks later. If the lunar eclipse happens first, then a solar eclipse will follow two weeks later. In six months the pattern repeats. Solar and lunar eclipses are the most important New and Full Moon cycles to pay attention to in your chart. You will be shown in Chapter 6 how to find all of the New and Full Moon cycles occurring in your chart. You will learn how to figure their positions every month by reading the sign positions of the New and Full Moons in the daily calendar.

Another section shows you when the planets are visible in the morning and evening sky. How can you tell the difference between a star and a planet? Stars twinkle because the air currents in the Earth's atmosphere distort their incoming light. Planets are visible because of the steady reflected sunlight off their surface. Venus is the brightest planet, sometimes referred to incorrectly as the morning or evening "star." Jupiter is the next brightest planet. Of the visible planets, Mercury is the most difficult to see because it is always close to the sun at sunrise or sunset.

On the same page is a chart that lists the dates of visible meteor showers. They are always on the same dates each year. The earth passes through bands of meteors (pieces of space rock) that look like shooting stars when they burn up upon entering the Earth's atmosphere. The friction with the air causes them to burn. The biggest meteor showers average at least fifty meteors an hour.

Sometimes a meteor storm will occur and you can see up to several hundred an hour. I have sometimes seen a meteor explode into two or three pieces, leaving white vapor trails behind them. Once when I was up about ten thousand feet in the mountains, I saw what is called a fireball. It trailed a blue-white vapor before exploding into three pieces, lighting up the whole forest, nearby mountains, and snowfields like a flashbulb for only a second before darkness returned. I could not hear it, but what a spectacular sight to witness! Meteors are really fun to watch. Take a lounge chair in warm weather and get away from city lights. In the winter bundle up or look out the window of your car.

In the rare instances when a meteor hits the earth, it is called a meteorite. A large crater caused by the impact of a meteorite can be seen near Flagstaff, Arizona. If a large enough meteorite hits the earth it can cause considerable damage. A large meteorite, maybe a small asteroid, is one theory of what might have caused the extinction of the dinosaurs. The huge impact would have caused so much smoke in the atmosphere that photosynthesis could no longer take place. All plant life would have died, as well as the creatures that depended upon plants to live.

Turn your attention to the section "Signs of the Zodiac." Your Sun, Moon, and Rising Sign are the three most important factors of your chart. Your Rising sign is the sign at 9 o'clock in your natal chart. I recommend you begin by reading the qualities of the signs that are your Sun, Moon, and Rising Sign. You can start absorbing the material and begin working with it. Reading about a friend's or your spouse's three primary signs will also help you learn the meaning of the signs. Notice that beside each of the signs is a glyph. Focus at first on learning the names of the signs. Knowing the glyphs is another translation that will happen as you proceed through the *Celestial Guide*®.

The next section is "Moon through the Signs." You will be referring to this section frequently. Every 2½ days the Moon changes signs. You can get a quick astrological reference point by looking up what sign the Moon is in for any particular day. This information is indicated by the sign's glyph in the upper right hand corner for the day. You can find the sign the glyph refers to in the "Moon through the Signs" section. Reading the Moon sign each day will be part of the repetition that will help you remember the sign qualities.

To reinforce learning the qualities of each sign, read the "Signs of the Zodiac" section for whatever sign the Moon is in each day. If the day's Moon sign is Aquarius, review "Moon in Aquarius" and then read about the sign of Aquarius in the "Signs of the Zodiac" section. It is preferable to do this in the morning, so that you can keep some of the sign's qualities in mind for the day. Be aware of the ways in which those sign qualities show up for you throughout the day.

Knowing what sign the Moon is in will also help you interpret the symbolism of your dreams. Your dreams for any particular night can have an interpretation based on the characteristics of what sign the Moon is in that night. In other words, whatever sign the Moon is in on the night you are dreaming will be a symbolic reference point for interpreting the meaning of your dreams. If the Moon changes signs on a given night, then you are going to be influenced by two signs instead of one. The symbolic language for each sign will be discussed in Chapter 4.

Remember that when you look at the Moon at night its position will be backward almost one constellation from the daily position recorded in the *Celestial Guide®* and the planetary tables at the end of the Guide. As mentioned earlier, the constellations of astronomy are a different system than the zodiac of tropical astrology.

The next section, "Moon Void of Course" refers to the Moon's course through the zodiac. It goes around the wheel of your chart once every 28 days. Every 2½ days, before it moves into the next sign, the Moon goes "Void of Course." During this time, it is in a kind of no-man's land between the sign it left and the one it is entering. During this time, the magnetic field necessary for the Moon to activate anything into your life is void, null. There is no energy for positive or negative events to happen. Sometimes this lasts just a few minutes, but I have seen it last for nearly 48 hours.

This period of time is very important to be aware of, not only for yourself, but everyone else, especially if you are self-employed dealing with appointments and schedules. During a Moon Void of Course time it is best to avoid making decisions and starting any new project or direction, including beginning a journey. If you attempt to do things during Moon Void of Course, it will be like digging for clams at high tide—you are not going to find any. Moon Void of Course will be explained in detail in Chapter 2.

The next section is called "Planets." The first chart you see there gives the planet's name, followed by its glyph. To the right is a column with the heading "Rulership." Each planet has what is called a home sign; some have two home signs. These home signs are called a planet's sign of rulership. It is important to know the signs of rulership, especially for the visible planets (Sun through Saturn on the list). The strongest sign(s) for each planet's energy is expressed in its sign of rulership.

For instance, the Sun's home sign is Leo. The Sun is in Leo during most of the month of August, the hottest month of the year in the Northern Hemisphere. This association can help you remember what the hottest planet's home, or ruling sign, is. The next planet listed is the Moon; its home sign is Cancer. Every month the Moon travels through its home sign of Cancer. Every year the Sun, Mercury, Venus, and sometimes Mars travel through their home signs. (Note that Mercury, Venus, and Mars have two home signs.) You will find this information useful as you track the planets' path through the zodiac in any given year.

The next column is "Key Words," which indicates the major qualities associated with each planet. Below this chart the planets are listed by name, followed by their symbol, or glyph. Each planet has a description of its qualities and function. Mercury has a special section titled "Mercury Retrograde" followed by the glyph for Mercury and a symbol for retrograde that looks like a prescription symbol. Remember retrograde refers to the apparent backward motion of a planet through the zodiac.

Why does Mercury retrograde have its own section while none of the other planets are listed with their retrograde description? Mercury retrograde is one cycle to definitely watch for and keep track of in the *Celestial Guide*®. Mercury's influence includes your mental faculties and communication. When it goes retrograde communications and the media can get flipped around more than usual, sometimes much more than usual.

Its retrograde cycle is just as important to keep track of as the New and Full Moons and Void of Course cycles. Mercury goes retrograde three times each year for three weeks.

The "Aspects" section covers the planets' angular relationships with each other. These will be explored in Chapter 6. Next "The Lunar Cycle" section covers the New Moon, First Quarter, Full Moon, and Last Quarter Moon transitions. This is the second most important section to understand after "Moon Void of Course." The Lunar Cycle will be covered in detail in Chapter 2.

Following the main body of the daily calendar are monthly planetary tables showing the positions of the planets, which are listed by glyph at the top of ten columns. In the far-left column labeled "day," each month's dates are listed and the four phases of the Moon are indicated. The darkened Moon face is the New Moon. A week later the First Quarter Moon is shown with the darkened left half of the Moon. A week later the Full Moon is drawn as a lighted happy face. In another week the symbol for the Last Quarter Moon is drawn with the right half darkened.

You can use this section as a quick reference for the month. Each page shows what signs the planets are in for any given day of the month and whether they are going direct or retrograde. You might find it helpful to write out the planets' names above or next to their glyphs to make it easier to read until you learn the glyphs.

At the top of each planetary column, beneath the glyph for the planet, is the symbol for which sign the planet is in. The sign is located between the numbers for the degrees and minutes for the first day of the month. The left number in the column is the degree of the sign that the planet is in, and the right number in the column is the minutes of a degree for the planet. There are sixty minutes in a degree just like there are sixty minutes in an hour.

If a planet changes signs during the month, the new sign is indicated lower in the column beside the appropriate date. The Moon changes signs every two to three days so it will have all 12 signs listed in its column. The Sun moves about a degree a day, so it moves about 30° in a month, changing signs around the 21st of each month. An astrological month is from about the 21st of one month to about the 21st of the next month. Leap year throws these dates off each year by up to two days. Remember from the first chart of planetary motions that the inner planets move faster than the outer planets.

You will notice the letter R at the beginning of one or more shaded columns. This indicates when a planet goes retrograde and for how long—as long as you see the gray shaded area. The only two planets that do not go retrograde are the Sun and Moon.

Now go to the far right column and find the symbol for Pluto. Remember how short Pluto's orbit appears in the "Planetary Motion" section? Here in the planetary tables you will see that in a whole month Pluto moves a degree or less. As you can see from the columns, the outer planets move more slowly, the further away they are from the Sun.

The planets are always in motion. They activate your natal planets in cycles called transits. The planets Sun, Mercury, Venus, and Mars will activate a planet in your natal chart from one to three days. The planets Jupiter through Pluto will activate a planet in your natal chart from one week to four weeks, or more. The outer planets make you aware of them for a longer period of time than the inner planets. The slower a planet moves through the zodiac the more thorough will be the changes it brings into your life when its transits activate a planet in your natal chart.

Following the planetary tables, some calendars have a table giving the positions of asteroids, including Chiron. These are not planets, but fragmented pieces of space rock. Some astrologers use them and others do not. The asteroid belt is the debris of an exploded planet that used to orbit between Mars and Jupiter. The four major asteroids listed in the table are Ceres, Pallas, Juno, and Vesta followed by Chiron, which is an asteroid orbiting between Saturn and Uranus. I will focus on the planets only, since they are the major players on the stage of your life.

Toward the back of the *Celestial Guide®* is a chart called "Table of Ascendants," which is good for any year. If you have someone's birth time, date, and place of birth you can guess fairly closely within two signs what their Rising Sign might be. If you have a computer program, then you can get the exact Rising Sign. On the inside back cover of the book is a table of sunrise and sunset times and instructions on how to compute them.

Before proceeding with an explanation of the Lunar Cycle, I want to give you a brief orientation of our position in the galaxy. We are in the Milky Way galaxy, which looks like a spiral, about 2/3 of the way from its center. You can see the Milky Way as a band of stars going from north to south through the Northern Cross. You are actually looking toward the center of the galaxy where the most stars congregate. We are traveling at about 18 miles a second, so fasten your seat belts! The Sun is actually taking us with it around the center of the galaxy, a 250 million year journey. The Hubbell telescope has discovered that there are millions upon millions of galaxies out there with trillions upon trillions of stars in each one. What are the chances that life might be found in any one of those star systems that have planets? Mind boggling, is it not?

[1] Another system is called the sidereal zodiac. It is used by astrologers called siderealists or Vedic astrologers and is based on the constellations of astronomy as they are seen in a star chart, rather than on the first day of spring, which is within one day of the same date every year. When the ancients first wrote down the zodiac, the first day of spring was in the constellation of Aries. But, because of the Earth's wobble on its axis, the constellations of astronomy on which the sidereal wheel is based shift one degree backward through the zodiac every 72 years. The constellations have moved about 24 degrees on the first day of spring since the zodiac system was handed down to us. Therefore, the sidereal wheel is now different from the one that I am using as the tropical zodiac wheel. Right now in the sidereal system, the first day of spring points almost toward the beginning of the constellation of Pisces. It has been argued that these two systems are contradictory and therefore astrology charts are unreliable. The two systems of plotting the planets' positions are a frame of reference, and each is accurate within its frame of reference.

Chapter 2

THE LUNAR CYCLE

To understand the influence of the planets in our lives and how to apply that information to daily living, it is important to understand the Lunar Cycle. The Moon acts as the trigger for propelling the planets' electromagnetic fields into our lives. It works something like the movement of the second hand on a clock. The Moon creates a shift with each movement.

For an understanding of the Lunar Cycle, it is important to know how to read and interpret the Moon Void of Course influence. In the upper right hand corner of October 16 (Figure 2), note the symbol of a crescent shaped Moon followed by the symbol (v/c) and a time. This is the time on that date that the Moon goes Void of Course, given in Pacific and/or Eastern Time.

In the lower right-hand section of the Void of Course day, a planetary alignment called an aspect is listed at the time of the Void of Course period. A crescent Moon followed by an aspect symbol to a planet is shown for the same time as the v/c time given above.

Figure 2

	Eastern	Pacific
FRIDAY 6	☽v/c 5:13a ☽→♎ 10:01p	☽v/c 2:13a ☽→♎ 7:01p
Kirk Kerkorian 1917 Alexander Pushkin 1799	☽✱♃ 5:13a ☉✱♅ 7:20a	☽✱♃ 2:13a ☉✱♅ 4:20a

	Eastern	Pacific
SATURDAY 7	☽ in ♎	☽ in ♎

The Void of Course time starts when the Moon makes its last alignment in its current sign to another planet before moving into the next sign. The Moon stays Void of Course (v/c) until it moves into the next sign. The time that it will move into the next sign is given immediately below the v/c information and is indicated by another crescent shaped Moon, followed by a horizontal arrow pointing to the glyph of the next sign and the time it enters that sign (Figure 2). If you do not see the Crescent Moon with the arrow pointing to the next sign on the day of the v/c time, then look at the next day for the symbol of its sign change. In rare instances of extra long v/c times, you may have to look two days ahead to find the time of the change. When the Moon is Void of Course over 24 hours you might feel a general tension in the air. People tend to be somewhat more edgy, maybe because something they are trying to do or purchases they have made are not working out the way they had hoped or expected.

Moon Void of Course influence relates to initiating something, not carrying it out. (Note Maynard's comments on v/c regarding the success, or rather the lack thereof, of presidential candidates who were nominated while the Moon was Void of Course.) If you schedule appointments during a Void of Course time, track the energy to see how the appointment turns out. After making an appointment during Moon Void of Course I have had people walk in a half-hour late, three hours late, or even think their appointment was on a different day than agreed upon. A client called me late one night saying it was an emergency; that he must see me at once for a reading. The Moon happened to be Void of Course so I scheduled the appointment for the next morning. The appointment time came and went. The person did not show up, nor did he call to tell me that he had canceled the appointment in his mind. Note that holding a session during Moon Void of Course is different than making the appointment to have the session during Moon Void of Course.

Two cycles of the Moon are described in "The Lunar Cycle" section of the *Celestial Guide*®. One cycle is the sidereal period of about 27½ days. The other is the synodic period of about 29½ to 30 days. The difference between these cycles is about 2½ days or 60 hours, corresponding to the pre-New Moon period.

Remember that the Earth is revolving around the Sun while the Moon is revolving around the Earth. The time the Moon takes to complete one cycle through the zodiac from its previous New Moon position to the same point in the zodiac is about 27½ days. The Earth has now moved with the Moon about 30° around the Sun since that last New Moon (Figures 3 and 4). The Moon now has to "catch up" with the Sun-Earth alignment, which is already in a different sign. It takes the Moon about 2½ days to travel this "extra distance" so that it is again between the Sun and Earth, as a New Moon, in the same degree of the zodiac as the Sun (Figures 3 and 4). Every month the Moon has to play "catch up" to be between the Earth and the Sun because of the Earth's orbit around the Sun. This "catch up" time is called the pre-New Moon cycle.

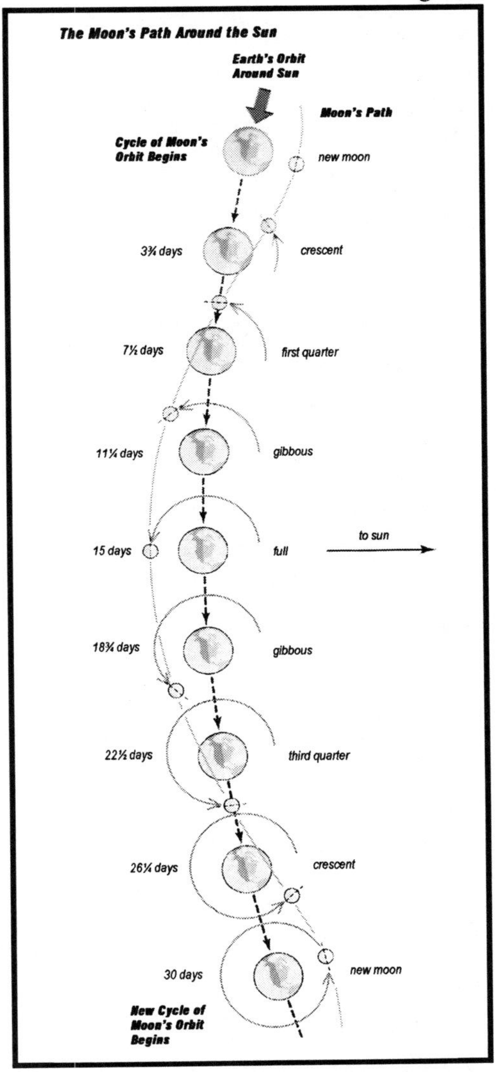

Figure 3

This "catch up" time is considered a "rest" time for the Moon. At the point of completing its sidereal cycle (27½ days) the Moon has completed its journey from seeding time back to its previous seeding time. This is the time the Moon has expended its growth and nurturing energy from being fertilized with the solar seed of the last New Moon. The Moon now "rests" magnetically while it catches up to its next New Moon position. It lies barren and infertile before receiving the next sign's New Moon seeding from the Sun. At the New Moon it receives the new solar seed from the Sun to bear fruit at the next Full Moon.

The pre-New Moon period of 2½ days or 60 hours before the New Moon functions like a Void of Course time. The information in the section "Moon Void of Course" also applies to the pre-New Moon period. If you start something new like a relationship, apply for a job, or initiate a project, you are in a kind of null zone for the Moon's energy. This pre-New Moon period also signals the end of development or completion time for any situation you started at the previous New Moon. You may notice that you require more rest and sleep during this pre-New Moon period.

Figure 4

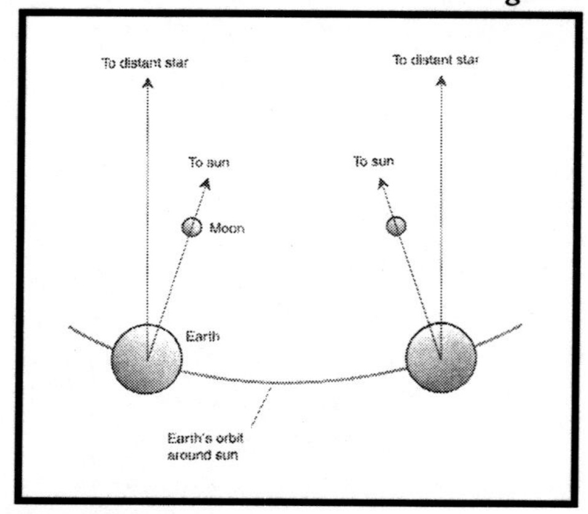

An easy way to figure this period of 2½ days or 60 hours is to look up the time of the New Moon. Say it is at 6:00 PM Friday. Go back 24 hours, which puts you at 6:00 PM the previous day (Thursday). Continue another 24 hours back and you are at 6:00 PM two days previous (Wednesday) for a total of 48 hours. Now subtract the additional 12 hours, which takes you to 6:00 AM Wednesday, giving you a total of 2½ days or sixty hours before the New Moon at 6:00 AM on Friday. You will always have the same hour and minute sixty hours before the New Moon time, only a PM time will change to AM, or if the New Moon time is AM it will change to PM.

Within the main body of the daily *Celestial Guide®* you will find a symbol for the Moon's phase displayed in the upper right-hand corner of the date of the exact lunar phase. To the right of the image you are told which phase of the Moon happens on that day, such as New Moon or Full Moon. Just below these words you are told what sign that phase of the Moon is in. The glyph for the sign is between numbers indicating the degrees and minutes, displayed in the same manner in which they are displayed in the planetary column in the back of the *Celestial Guide®*. Below this is the time of the lunar phase in Eastern or Pacific Time.

The Lunar Cycle repeats every 30 days. About every 30 days from the new Moon another new Moon occurs. About every 30 days from the Full Moon another Full Moon occurs. In 30 days another Quarter Moon will appear just like the Quarter Moon appearing four weeks before. The Lunar Cycle occurs because the Moon rises about 55 minutes later each day, causing the cycle to progress (Figures 5 and 6).

The day of the New Moon is the one day that you cannot see the Moon because the dark half faces the Earth. If you could orbit the Moon around to its other side, you would see the Full Moon facing the Sun.

Figure 5

Half the Moon is facing toward you. The other half of the Moon is facing away from you. The New Moon is in the same degree of the zodiac in the sky as the Sun.

The First Quarter Moon appears due south halfway between the two

Figure 6

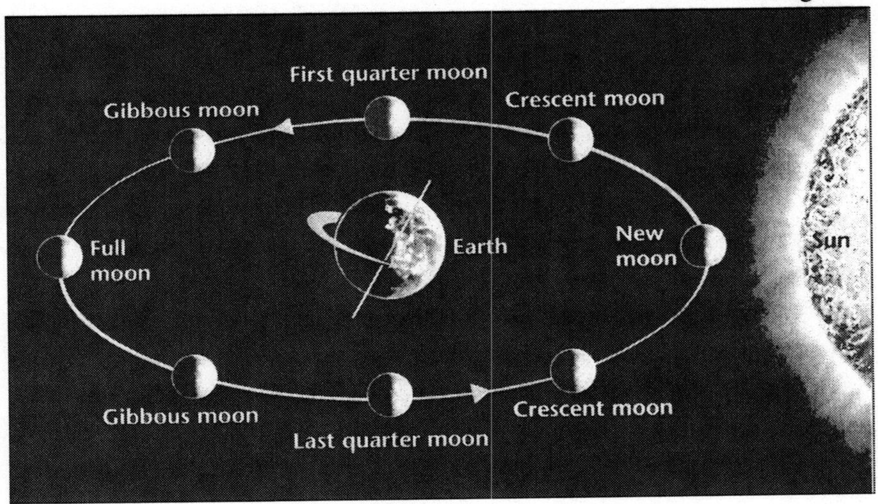

horizons at sunset. In two weeks if you get up at sunrise the lit half will be reversed due south. You will see the other half of the Moon with the lighted half facing toward sunrise. The half you see at the First Quarter Moon would be dark while the dark half would be light in two weeks. That half-lit Moon is called the Last Quarter Moon. If you divide the sphere of the Moon into four equal parts you see that only a quarter of the sphere is really visible to you (Figures 5 and 6).

The New Moon is a seeding time of new beginnings. The window of time to optimize starting something new—such as a relationship, a business endeavor, or a trip—is within 60 hours or 2½ days after the New Moon. Watch for anything new coming into your life especially during this period. In the "Aspect" section of the *Celestial Guide®* is an entry written as "Moon conjunct the Sun (New Moon)" with an explanation afterward. Read this section for additional information about the importance of the New Moon time.

It is important to know the sign of the New and Full Moons (Figures 7 and 8). When you know the sign you can identify the qualities of the sign. Once you identify the qualities of a sign, you can align with those qualities, since they are in the collective unconscious of all of us. You can strengthen the qualities of the sign of the New and Full Moon in yourself by being conscious of them each month. You can tune into their energies and align your intentions with the qualities of the sign. (See Chapters 7 and 8.) Your life will be more imbued with the energy of the New and Full Moon sign because you imprinted into yourself the energy of that sign.

Note what sign the New Moon is in because that sign's influence sets the theme for the next four weeks. Every New Moon cycle lasts four weeks in whatever sign it occurs. Read about the monthly sign of the New Moon in the front of the *Celestial Guide®* under the sections "Moon through the Signs" and "Signs of the Zodiac." The theme for four weeks is rooted in the sign of the New Moon even after it moves out of that sign. The Moon changes signs every 2½ days.

For instance, I traveled into a wilderness area knowing that the New Moon was also a Solar Eclipse in Leo. Leo represents one's identity and children. I did a meditation with the Leo energy representing my identity, my Spirit, my authority, my relationship with my father, my relationship to being a father—all qualities of Leo. I sat down to do a meditation and began speaking out loud about these subjects. With my hands outstretched to the sunset, I gave thanks to the forces there for allowing me to be there. An energy came through—maybe from my Spirit—and I channeled a prayer that I intended to seat in my consciousness with that Leo New Moon. I began with a prayer of appreciation and ended up say-

Figure 7

	Eastern	Pacific
FRIDAY 27	New Moon 5♋37 4:08a	New Moon 5♋37 1:08a
	☽ in ♋	☽ in ♋
		☽☌☉ 1:08a
		☽△♆ 4:53a
	☽☌☉ 4:08a	☽☍♇ 2:39p
Helen Keller 1880	☽△♆ 7:53a	☽□♅ 10:16p
Khloé Kardashian 1984	☽☍♇ 5:39p	☽△♄ 11:48p
SATURDAY 28	☽ in ♋	☽ in ♋
	☽v/c 9:03p	☽v/c 6:03p

Figure 8

	Eastern	Pacific
		☽✶♆ 8:12a
		☽☌♇ 3:48p
E.B. White 1899	☽✶♆ 11:12a	☽□♅ 10:45p
Rachael Taylor 1984	☽☌♇ 6:48p	☽✶♄ 11:07p
SATURDAY 12	Full Moon 20♑03 7:25a	Full Moon 20♑03 4:25a
	☽v/c 9:56p	☽v/c 6:56p
	☽→♒ 11:07p	☽→♒ 8:07p
	☽□♅ 1:45a	
	☽✶♄ 2:07a	☽☍☉ 4:25a
	☽☍☉ 7:25a	☽□♂ 9:42a
Van Cliburn 1934	☽□♂ 12:42p	☽☍♃ 6:56p
Malala Yousafzai 1997	☽☍♃ 9:56p	☿→♋ 9:45p
SUNDAY 13	☽ in ♒	☽ in ♒

ing things I needed to speak as my intentions for ten to fifteen minutes. It was one of the most profound experiences of my life, which I was still integrating four weeks afterwards.

The Quarter Moons are important juncture points in the Lunar Cycle. Read the *Celestial Guide*® entry for "Moon square Sun (First or Last Quarter)." The First Quarter is a development part of the Lunar Cycle when energy is growing with the increasing light of the waxing Moon and maturing toward the fruition time of the Full Moon. At the First Quarter Moon the seed of what you planted at a previous New Moon time—not necessarily the most recent New Moon—will appear in your life and become visible in some way, like a sprout pushing its way through the surface of the Earth. The influence lasts about 12 hours before and after the exact time of the Quarter Moon (Figure 9). Round off the Quarter Moon time to the nearest half-hour for simpler figuring. For instance, if the Quarter Moon is at 9:00 AM, then look for its influence from about 9:00 PM the previous day to 9:00 PM that same day. Note any significant events during this time as likely part of the New or Full Moon cycle that precedes the Quarter Moon.

If this sprout is something that you really desire, you nurture it as you would a flower or a fruit tree. You water it, give it some fertilizer, and maybe even talk or sing to it. But if weeds have come up and you are wondering what they are doing in your garden of life, the First Quarter Moon time is the best time to pull those weeds out. What does a weed's taproot do? It grows down fast, usually outstripping the other desirable plants. If any issues or challenges come up for you at the First Quarter

Figure 9

Ann Landers 1918	☽⚹♃ 0:21a	
U.S. Independence Day	☉☍♇ 4:00a	☉☍♇ 1:00a
SATURDAY	**Eastern**	**Pacific**
5	First Qtr 13♎24 7:59a	First Qtr 13♎24 4:59a
	☽ in ♎	☽ in ♎
	☽□♇ 5:47a ☽□☉ 7:59a ☽△♀ 9:52a ☽☍♅ 1:46p ☽☌♂ 9:31p	☽□♇ 2:47a ☽□☉ 4:59a ☽△♀ 6:52a ☽☍♅ 10:46a ☽☌♂ 6:31p
P.T. Barnum 1810 Rich "Goose" Gossage 1951		
SUNDAY	**Eastern**	**Pacific**
6	☽v/c 11:31a ☽→♏ 3:34p	☽v/c 8:31a ☽→♏ 12:34p

Moon time, those are the weeds to pay attention to. The weeds are trying to get the nutrients of your attention as well as your constructive ideas. Pull out the weeds by resolving to the greatest degree possible whatever conflicts and tensions are present. Whatever alignments a New Moon has made in your chart will come to the surface of your life experiences at the First Quarter Moon time.

The New Moon begins beneath the surface of the earth as a seed (Figure 10-1). At the First Quarter the seed sprouts through the surface (Figure 10-2). Cultivate and encourage what you desire during the First Quarter and deal with what you do not desire as if you were pulling out the weeds.

What will happen at the Full Moon if you do not pull the weeds out? Look at Figure 10-3 with the Full Moon over the Earth at maximum growth, symbolized as the potential crop of what was seeded at a New Moon time. If you did not pull the weeds by the First Quarter Moon time, their taproots are taking the water and nutrients from what you desired to cultivate. A lot more effort will now be required to eradicate the weeds from your life. Make a strong effort to get rid of any weeds that remain at the Full Moon time. If they are not pulled by the Full Moon

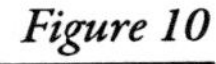

Figure 10

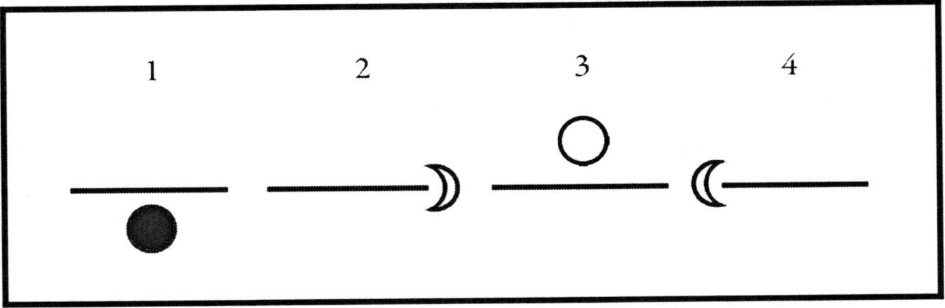

time then you will likely have a disintegrating kind of energy rather than a unifying kind of energy during the remaining twelve days of the Moon's waning cycle.

Once the Full Moon occurs it ushers in another cycle lasting two weeks. Note what sign the Full Moon is in because that sign's influence for two weeks now joins the New Moon's influence. Every Full Moon cycle lasts two weeks in whatever sign it occurs. Read about the monthly sign of the Full Moon in the front of the *Celestial Guide®* under the sections "Moon Through the Signs" and "Signs of the Zodiac." The theme of the sign of the Full Moon is activated even after it moves out of that sign, just as the sign for the New Moon continues as noted before.

The last entry in the "Aspect" section of the *Celestial Guide®* is written as "Moon Opposite Sun (Full Moon)." This period can be either a unifying or a separating time. An opposition is really a polarity. When you take two magnets and put both poles facing each other they repel each other—you cannot put them together. However, if you turn one of the magnets around, they pull together as a result of their attraction to each other; you have to use strong force to pull them apart. The is polarity. Opposition is really a polarity, like light and dark, male and female, spirit and material. The energies of planets do not have to be in opposition—they can be complementary. Opposition can either be attracting or repelling, depending on your inner polarity with the life situations in which you find yourself at that time.

If you have an attraction going at the Full Moon you will have a great time as a couple. But if you have an opposition going you will have antagonism between you and your partner. The police are busier around the Full Moon, as are emergency rooms and other medical staff at the hospital. More babies are born during a Full Moon. I have done a study of the major earthquakes and volcanoes of the 20th century and almost all of them happened within two or three days of New and Full Moons.

Seven days after the Full Moon, the Last Quarter Moon finds the fruit dropping to the ground as in Figure 10-4. The Last Quarter Moon will be due south of you at sunrise. The influence lasts about 12 hours before and after the exact time of the Last Quarter Moon, the same length of time as the First Quarter Moon's influence (Figure 11). Now is the time to take inventory of the fruit you have in the storehouse.

Questions to ask yourself are:

1) What is in your inventory of the last three weeks?

2) Does anything need to be cleaned up?

3) Where is your project going?

Figure 11

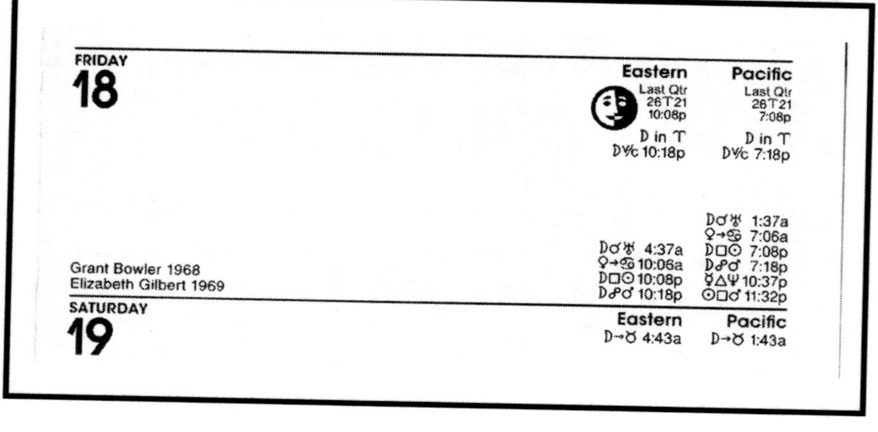

FRIDAY
18

	Eastern	Pacific
	Last Qtr 26♈21 10:08p	Last Qtr 26♈21 7:08p
	☽ in ♈ ☽v/c 10:18p	☽ in ♈ ☽v/c 7:18p
	☽☌♅ 4:37a ♀→♋ 10:06a ☽□☉ 10:08p ☽☍♂ 10:18p	☽☌♅ 1:37a ♀→♋ 7:06a ☽□☉ 7:08p ☽☍♂ 7:18p ☿△♆ 10:37p ☉□♂ 11:32p

Grant Bowler 1968
Elizabeth Gilbert 1969

SATURDAY
19

	Eastern	Pacific
	☽→♉ 4:43a	☽→♉ 1:43a

4) How fruitful or dysfunctional have the last three weeks been?

5) Is the harvest of your storehouse plentiful or lean with slim pickings and sour fruit that should be thrown out? The bad apple can spread decay and rot into future New Moon cycles if it is not discarded.

6) What new insights have you gained?

7) What should you now be aware of in the coming cycles?

8) Has the ground you have been standing on been shaken up?

9) What adjustments would be good to make as course corrections?

From the Last Quarter Moon you prepare for the seedtime of the next New Moon. What are you preparing for the New Moon that will be coming in another week? With the Moon, everything happens every seven days.

If the New or Full Moon is in your Sun, Moon, or Rising Sign, then you will more strongly experience the qualities of that sign during the corresponding lunar cycle since you were born with an affinity for that sign in your birth chart. If an eclipse happens in your Sun, Moon or Rising Sign then the qualities of that sign will be more strongly emphasized than if there was only a normal New or Full Moon.

During each Lunar Cycle keep track of any important events like phone calls, checks in the mail, disappointments, rerouting schedules, relationships—anything you think is important. Write the event down on the day of its occurrence in the *Celestial Guide®* and see if it is related or connected to the sign of the New or Full Moon. Your experiences of what happened will help explain what is occurring in the calendar, just like the saying, "as above, so below." Your journal is the best way to learn astrology because you will have the experience to connect with the astrological information, combining your left and right brain.

The highest tides are around the New and Full Moons. The least difference between the tides is at the Quarter Moons. Your body is made up of about 80% water and responds to the magnetics controlling the tides. Water responds to emotional and mental imprinting, as Dr. Masaru Emoto's brilliant photos show from his *Messages from Water* series. The New and Full Moons are therefore excellent times to reprogram your unconscious by writing and saying affirmations. (See Chapters 7 and 8).

If you fast for 24 hours a day before or the day of a New or Full Moon, you are working with the tidal rhythms of the Moon to cleanse your body of toxins. The New or Full Moon in Virgo is a good time to fast because Virgo is the healing sign for cleansing and purification.[1]

What you suggest to yourself before going to sleep on the nights of the New and Full Moons can also assist you in aligning your unconscious with the sign. Set and reinforce your intentions, especially as you go to sleep. What you sleep on is magnified during the night. If you go to sleep mad at your partner, you will tend to wake up with the anger even stronger. If you go to sleep at peace with your partner, you will tend to wake up with an angel beside you! Setting a tone of peace within your sense of self for your sleep time is important. The tone you go to sleep with also affects your dreams. Upon awakening it is very important to set the tone of your day, even if you only take a minute or two to do it. You are energetically reminding yourself to stay connected to Source throughout your day.

Another practical application of the Moon's Lunar Cycle is connected to your hair. If you desire to promote the growth of your hair, cut it around the New Moon. If you desire more body and style, have your hair styled around the Full Moon. If you want your permanent to last longer or your hair has difficulty staying in a permanent, have you hair done while the Moon is in the fixed earth sign of Taurus.

If you desire to have your lawn grow more quickly, cut it during the waxing Moon, from New to Full Moon. If you desire your lawn to grow more slowly, cut it while the Moon is waning—two days after the Full Moon to three days before the New Moon.

Eclipses are the most prominent New and Full Moon cycles. A Solar Eclipse intensifies the energy of a New Moon because the Sun, Moon, and Earth are in an exact alignment, forming a straight line (Figure 12). The Moon actually crosses the face of the Sun, blocking out its light, which causes night for a few minutes wherever the shadow crosses the Earth. The stars even appear. The longest Solar Eclipse I experienced lasted over seven minutes on the Big Island of Hawaii.

The relative distances from Earth to the Moon and Sun make both spheres look like they are the same diameter, even though the Sun is actually much, much larger. The Moon is approximately 240,000 miles away from the Earth while the Sun is about 93 million miles away. The Sun is approximately 400 times bigger than the Moon, but it is also about 400 times further away from Earth than the Moon, which accounts for both orbs looking as if they are the same size.

Have you ever taken a magnifying glass and burned a leaf or piece of paper? Similarly, a Solar Eclipse is like a laser light coming into your psyche. A Solar Eclipse casts a narrow shadow across the Earth's surface for only a few minutes. It affects the whole Earth because its effect goes down to the core of the Earth where its electromagnetic field is generated.

In pictures of a Solar Eclipse you can see solar flares bursting out from the surface of the Sun. The solar flares tend to increase coinciding with the 11-year Sun spot cycle. The biggest solar flares are what cause the Northern and Southern Lights. The Northern Lights are worth a flight to Canada or Alaska. You have some heads-up time since they happen about 24 hours

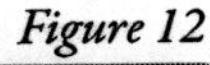

Figure 12

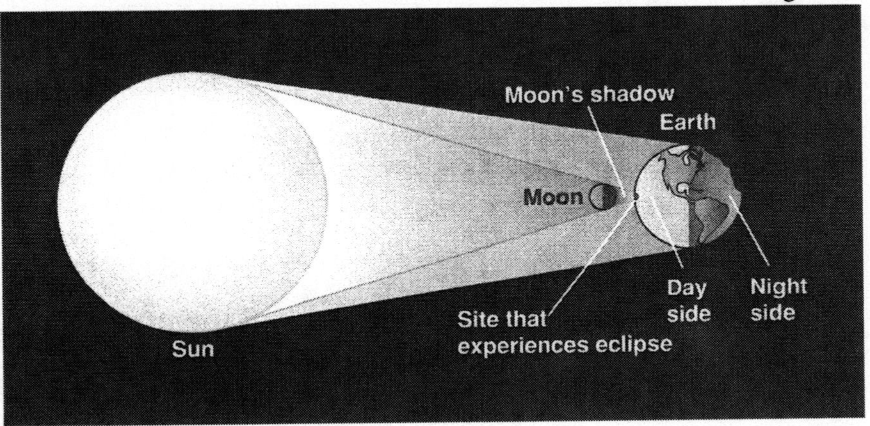

after a large solar flare is recorded. It takes that long for the solar wind to blow the highly charged particles into the Earth's magnetic field at the poles. The Northern Lights (Aurora Borealis) are the most phenomenal light show with wavy curtains and designs of violet, purple, green, and red light. I have even seen what looked like gold specks seemingly being flung across the heavens. It is an awesome sight!

The strongest Solar Eclipses are in the home signs of the Sun and Moon, which are Leo and Cancer respectively. Each planet has at least one home sign, called the ruling sign, where its influence is the strongest of all the other signs. (Ruling signs are discussed in detail in Chapter 3.) The next strongest influence of an eclipse is for one to occur in your Sun, Moon, or Rising Sign.

A Lunar Eclipse occurs because the Moon moves behind the Earth through its shadow, which takes several hours rather than several minutes, which is the case during a Solar Eclipse. The Full Moon is slowly enveloped by the shadow of the Earth (Figure 13). It either turns a deep maroon or disappears altogether, which allows you to see all the stars as if there were no Moon out. It then slowly reappears, coming out of the Earth's shadow to become a Full Moon again, lighting up everything with silver moonlight.

Why does the Moon turn maroon? The Sun's light actually travels through the Earth's atmosphere, which filters out all light except the red band in the spectrum. Since red is the only color that can pass entirely through the atmosphere, that is the color you see reflected on the Moon during a Lunar Eclipse. Brilliant sunrises and sunsets happen because the red spectrum is the only color spectrum not absorbed by the atmosphere.

If a Lunar Eclipse occurs on the Full Moon day that day in the *Celestial Guide®* will be designated with a slightly darkened happy face. In the upper right hand corner of the day will be the words "Lunar Eclipse" with the words "Full Moon" immediately beneath them. If a Solar Eclipse is to occur, you will see pointed rays around the darkened face of the Moon.

Figure 13

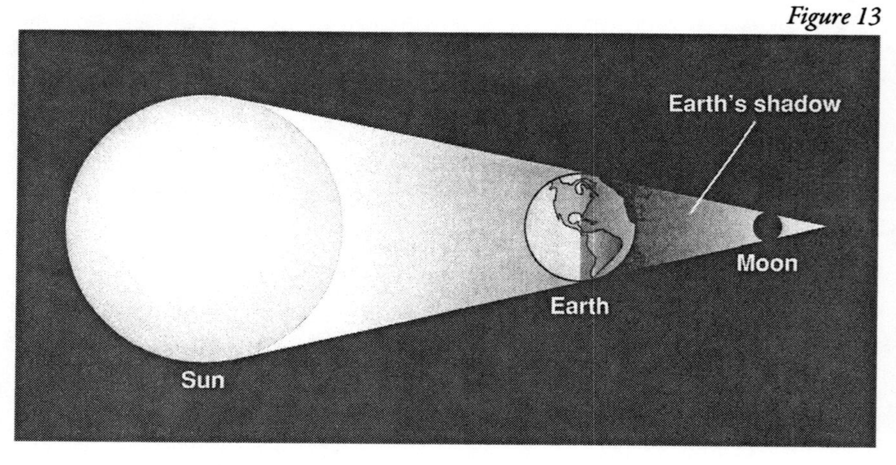

Above the words "New Moon" will be the words "Solar Eclipse."

If the Quarter Moon follows a Lunar or Solar Eclipse, then the window of its influence is about 24 hours (double the normal time) before and after the time of the Quarter Moon for a total of about 48 hours. If you are in an eclipse cycle and the time is about 9:00 AM Tuesday for the Quarter Moon, then the influence would be from about 9:00 AM on Monday to about 9:00 AM Wednesday.

If the Last Quarter Moon follows both a Solar and Lunar Eclipse keep in mind that it not only completes the Lunar Eclipse cycle of the previous week but also the Solar Eclipse cycle of the previous three weeks. You have a double emphasis of the 24-hour influence of whatever was going on in your chart with both solar and lunar eclipse energies. You can watch other people's lives respond to this influence as well. Remember that eclipse cycles happen in pairs twice a year, six months apart.

If your work involves frequent interaction with the public, these Quarter Moon times are important barometers for gauging your day. People will tend to be either more reactive or friendlier. If they are working through issues they will be more bristly. If life is going well for them, they will have a smile and a bounce to their step.

In Chapter 3, the energetic characteristics of each planet will be discussed.

[1] Health conditions may prevent some persons from fasting.

Chapter 3

THE PLANETS

Before we explore the energy of the planets, a brief background of my viewpoint of astrology is appropriate here.

I look at astrology as symbolism because it is based on symbols representing the 12 signs of the zodiac. I believe that if we look at our lives symbolically we can better understand our opportunities as well as our lessons. Our birth chart symbolizes both the potential strengths and weaknesses of the planetary magnetics that represent our life contracts and karma. The birth chart, as a schematic diagram, symbolizes unlimited potential for spiritual and emotional growth as we continually refine our energies up the cosmic octaves of evolution.

Remember that everything is energy. Whatever you act on and you agree with in your thoughts is imprinted with a signature code of your energy that goes out with that action or thought-form and returns it to you from the ocean of life. Thoughts that you agree with stay connected to your mind-field energy as a vibration. They stay connected to you energetically, as do your feelings and emotions.

Nothing about astrology is predetermined or fatalistic. All of your decisions and actions have a signature code that go out into the world encoded with the energy of your decision and action. The process is an impersonal law that has very personal results. Your beliefs and actions go out and "find" the corresponding situation and bring it back to you, like salmon returning to their spawning ground. The salmon, as your actions and decisions, go out to the ocean of life. Where do they return? To you—headquarters. Every action has an opposite and equal reaction. Every action you take comes back to roost with you.

The Golden Rule reminds you to treat others as you would like to be treated because that is exactly what happens. You are the cause and you receive the effect. You reap what you sow. Each of your actions has a reaction, which explains why there is an absolute order and justice in what happens in life. Everyone is under that law, just as everyone is under the law of gravity. If anything is predetermined, you determined it by your choices and actions. The planets do not do anything to you. They merely reflect back to you your beliefs and actions, just as they reflect sunlight.

Whether you hold onto fear thoughts or inspiring thoughts, those thoughts will go out as messengers into the ocean of life, and bring back to you the corresponding experience. For instance, most of us have felt guilty at one time or another to the degree that we want to punish ourselves. What does that guilt do? It returns punishment to us because we sent it out there to find our punishment. How many times do we punish ourselves before we say, "Hey, I've had enough of this"? Only then can we release the energy around our guilt. Our beliefs have the same impact as our actions. There is no such thing as an idle or a neutral thought.

A question that I have asked is: "When a person begins to pay attention to their intuition and starts to see an event that is coming toward them, how much of their seeing the event is actually creating it?" My answer is: "Everything!" They may not see (identify) the original cause of what is happening for them or to them, but they are creating the event.

I am describing how you interpret data and information—something I will discuss in more detail under Gemini and Mercury. Information is just data like your experiences or knowledge. But how you interpret that data has to do with Gemini and Mercury, which relate to the conscious mind. Your conscious mind is the knowledge of information as facts and figures—the computer files of your brain. The opposite sign, Sagittarius, represents the meaning that you give that knowledge and information.

How you perceive what is happening to you is very important. How you interpret your experience determines how you respond to what you perceive. I conduct a well-known psychology experiment with my astrology class. I take all of the students into another room and then bring Judy back to the classroom to tell her a two-minute story. I then have her stay in the room and have Susan come in. Judy tells Susan the story. Judy leaves the room and Susan stays. Then John comes in to hear the story from Susan. Five students and five stories later, I compare the last story told with the original. Of course, the last story is different from the original story because each student interpreted what he or she heard differently.

Each student hooked the information to something as a reference by association with what is familiar in his or her life about the story. The storytellers remembered what was important to them and that version of the story is what was passed on to the next person.

Another familiar example is that of three people witnessing an accident. They have three different versions of what happened because each person has selective perception and selective hearing. People tend to see what they want to see and hear what they want to hear.

Studies have shown that once the nervous system is conditioned and set in certain patterns, it will respond with the old programming, even though contrary data is coming into the brain. The brain literally overrides what is happening externally with old programming until we begin to question the validity of what we perceive as our experience. We can then change our ingrained perceptions through various healing processes. A distortion potential exists with all of the five senses, which is why it is useful to always question our perception of what is happening in our lives.

* * *

The planets are connected to the chakra system.[2] The chakras are bio-computers that pick up the energy fields of the planets. Every planet emits a different tone—a fact proven by astronomers. You cannot hear the tones, but the frequency can be multiplied up to the octaves of the audible range of humans. These tones activate the planets as aspects (Chapter 6) in your natal chart. Whatever is in your chakras that resonates to a planetary tone gets activated in your experience as opportunities or lessons.

Each planet reflects sunlight off its surface, imprinting/combining the light that comes to Earth with its own vibration or tone. Each tone emits a frequency which becomes expressed in the human experience.

Take for example two guitars with the same tuning positioned side by side. If I pluck the D string on the first guitar, the D string on the second guitar will sound, just not as loudly. Those strings are tuned to the same frequency, so they resonate with each other when one or the other is played. A planetary tone can resonate to energy in your chakras vibrating at a similar frequency, activating that energy into your experience.

An amazing example of this law was reported in the news about fires in Santa Barbara and Laguna Beach, CA. In the late summer these communities get what is called "sundowner winds" that blow downhill towards the ocean. If it is dry and there is a fire, the fire cannot be stopped. In the neighborhoods that were burnt to the ground, one or two houses built with the same materials were left standing, hardly touched by the flames even though they had been in the direct path of the fire. These houses may have had energy from the owners that did not resonate with fire burning them down.

Another example in the news cited a freeze in one of the southern states that wiped out all of the crops in the state. One farmer was interviewed because his field was the only one that did not freeze. He had no idea why. He told the news reporter that he prayed to God to protect his fields. He surmised that God must have done His job and protected them. The other farmers had their sprinklers on, just as he did, to protect their crops, but with a different unfortunate result.

Another story is about a retired man who walked into a café and approached a couple who were strangers to him. He asked them how much money they could use. Thinking he was joking, the husband off-handedly said, "Oh, $10,000." The older man wrote out a check to them for $10,000 right on the spot. When the couple took it to the bank they were shocked and pleasantly surprised to find out that they were $10,000 richer. Why did the man single this couple out from all other people in the café? What energy was being expressed as a resonance between the couple and the generous man?

Rulership

Return to the *Celestial Guide*®. Under the heading of "Planets" you will see a box listing each planet, the corresponding glyph, Rulership, and Key Words. Each planet has a home sign called its "Rulership." It is important to know the signs of rulership especially for the visible and faster moving planets, which are the Sun through Saturn. The signs of rulership are the strongest signs for each planet's energy to be expressed. A planet's energy is maximized while it is traveling through its ruling sign. Every month the Moon travels through its ruling sign of Cancer. Every year the Sun, Mercury, Venus, and sometimes Mars travel through their ruling signs. (Mercury, Venus, and Mars each have two ruling signs.)

Remember there are two places in the *Celestial Guide*® where you can find which sign a planet is in and what direction it is going. The first place is in the front of the *Celestial Guide*® under "Planetary Motions." The second place is in the back under the 12 months of planetary tables.

Once you know a planet's sign of rulership, you can refer to the chart at the beginning of the "Planets" section to learn its opposite sign of rulership. When a planet is in its opposite sign, it is similar to being a visitor in a foreign country. The opposite sign of a planet's rulership has traditionally been called its sign of detriment. I prefer to call it a compliant planet for that sign. Saying a planet is in detriment for a sign is an archaic label that has a detrimental, misleading connotation. To say the planet is compliant for a sign is akin to respecting and accepting wise counsel about observing and respecting the laws, customs, and rules of a foreign country. You can then avoid getting into difficulties with the local authorities and population while visiting there. You would not encounter detrimental situations in that country because you are compliant with honoring its laws and regulations.

By studying the characteristics of a planet and the characteristics of its compliant sign, you can see how the planet's energy can assist you to avoid clashing with the potential liabilities of that sign. By being compliant to the compliant planet's qualities, you can minimize, or eliminate altogether, potential or actual problems and conflicts inherent in a sign while the planet is in that compliant sign. You can mesh with a sign's assets by aligning to the compliant planet's strengths, just as you would adjust to the laws and customs of a foreign country so that you would not conflict with them. Likewise, you do not then become snared in a sign's liabilities.

Compliant signs for the planets:
Sun: Aquarius
Moon: Capricorn
Mercury: Sagittarius, Pisces
Venus: Aries, Scorpio
Mars: Taurus, Libra
Jupiter: Gemini, Virgo
Saturn: Cancer, Leo
Uranus: Leo
Neptune: Virgo
Pluto: Taurus

The Moon travels through its compliant sign of Capricorn once every month. Every year the Sun, Mercury, Venus, and sometimes Mars will travel through their compliant signs. Mercury, Venus, and Mars have two compliant signs.

Each planet also has an exalted sign for its expression. The opposite sign of exaltation has been traditionally called the sign of fall, which has an implied adverse archaic meaning. Instead of using the label "fall" for a sign, I prefer the word "receptive". The receptive sign is opposite its exalted sign. Like a planet's compliant sign, if you are receptive to the receptive planet's strengths you can minimize, or eliminate altogether, potential or actual problems and conflicts inherent in a sign while the planet is in that receptive sign. You can align with a sign's assets by aligning to the receptive planet's strengths. Receptive signs for the planets:

Sun: Libra
Moon: Scorpio
Mercury: Leo
Venus: Virgo
Mars: Cancer
Jupiter: Capricorn
Saturn: Aries
Uranus: Taurus
Neptune: Gemini
Pluto: Aquarius

Associating a planet as the cause of experiencing a sign's liabilities is like saying the red light at an intersection caused the vehicle that ran the red light to have an accident. A planet in a compliant or receptive sign emphasizes the potential of experiencing the sign's liabilities if we do not align with the planet's energy while it is there. However, if we do align with the planet's energy while in a compliant or receptive sign, we can experience harmony while the planet is there.

PERSONAL PLANETS

Symbolism of the Planets

The personal planets are the visible planets that extend out to Saturn. The transpersonal planets are the invisible planets: Uranus, Neptune, and Pluto. All planets generate only positive, constructive energy. When the signs are introduced in the next chapter, you will see that human choices and behavior determines how a planet's energy is expressed. The misapplication of the planets' energy is the result of human dysfunction and distortion of their energy, which is why signs have both positive and negative meanings. (Signs will be discussed in Chapter 4.)

The keywords for each planet are in italics. Delineating the keywords this way is meant to clear up ambiguous meanings for the planets when keywords are used for more than one planet in astrological literature.

SUN

The Sun is a star. The fusion process of the Sun creates *light.* If the Sun did not *shine*, you could not see the planets. You see the planets because of reflected sunlight, just as they reflect your karma (cause and effect) back to you.

As a star, the Sun shows where you tend to *shine* as the star on the stage of your life. It represents the *identity* of who you think you are, which involves just two choices—an ego or *authentic Self.* The ego is defined here as the false or separate self that is a substitute for your *authentic Self.* The ego, as a substitute self, can be the only other alternative to the *authentic Self.* The ego is separate from the *Light* of your *Spirit* and your *Divine Source*, whereas your *authentic Self* is connected to your *Spirit*, which is connected to your Divine *Source/Creator*.

If you *identify* with the ego as your self, you are going to act like an ego, which fosters arrogance, pride as superiority, and humiliation. The ego sets you up to be humiliated and humbled. The ego is always concerned with whom it is superior and inferior to. Issues of *authority* are connected to your Sun. The ego is always alert to who is a greater or lesser *authority*—a bigger or smaller ego—than it.

The Sun is where you go for the *source* of your *life*. If you understand your *Self* as being a *Spirit Being*, then you know your *source* of life comes from *Spirit*. *Spirit's Source* is the *Creator.* Who *created* you? If you *identify* with your *Self*, then you know you are a child of your *Creator*. You are connected to that *Source* for *Love*.

The *authentic Self* is always humble in its grandeur, so it does not experience being humbled through humiliation. It is at peace with itself and in harmony with others. It has no need to "prove" anything, and it does not feel threatened or lessened by the success of others. It is able to take pleasure in its own expression and to appreciate the expression of others.

The Sun is connected to your *heart* chakra, which *radiates* out as the *center* dynamo of all the chakras. It stays in a sign for 30 days. Anytime your Sun sign is activated by the planetary cycles, you will be making the decision of who you think you are.

MOON

Next is the Moon, which is associated with the *maternal, mother*. The Moon in your chart represents everything that makes up your *body*, except your skeleton, which is represented by Saturn. Who develops your *body* for you? Your *mother* who gave you birth. A spirit being requires a *body*—a form to live in on Earth. Developing a *body* involves you with four choices, which can be depicted by a triangle. At the top of the triangle you first choose a gender, followed by a race, and then a culture, in descending order. When you are born you become part of a family at the bottom of the triangle.

The Moon represents your *personality*—your *persona*. The family and home you were born into help to formulate your *personality* and create your sense of safety and security. Your Moon sign and any planets in the Moon's home sign of Cancer will indicate the degree to which you feel safe and secure on Earth.

The Moon also symbolizes the *body* and all of its functions of *instinct*. *Instincts* are feelings and autonomic reactions in humans and animals that support the survival of the species. They are passed on from generation to generation. We do not have to tell the *body* to carry on astounding, complex functions necessary for biological survival, such as digesting food and eliminating waste from cells. Functions of *instinct* also include the kind of information that causes a *mother* to know when her child needs her protection or help or an animal to sense danger.

My *instincts* to protect my *body* from potential harm were activated one time when I was walking along a trail. My *body instinctively* jumped about four feet off the trail before the sound of the coiled rattlesnake a few steps ahead registered in my brain.

The Moon is especially connected with fluids. It pulls on the *tides* as well as the *fluids* in people, plants, and animals. Associated with the reproductive cycle of *women*, the Moon also represents *fertility*. *Women* are well acquainted with the different *phases* of the Moon as it affects their monthly *moods* and *hormones*.

The moon stays in a sign for 2½ days. It is connected to the first chakra, which is located at the base of the sacrum.

MERCURY

The first planet out from the Sun is Mercury. Think of Mercury as a radio. It functions as the dual *messenger* planet of *communication. Communication* involves two processes. The first process is the speaker acting as a transmitter and clearly *communicating* what he/she intends to say. The second is a receiver listening to the *communication* in a way that they can interpret and comprehend it. You tune into a station transmitting someone talking and you listen through your radio's receiver, interpreting what you are hearing.

Your mind forms an energy that is divided into four parts, one of which is connected to Mercury as your *consciousness.*

Mercury is connected to the *throat chakra* of *communication* through speech, which activates thoughts into motion. One of the most powerful statements is to express gratitude for what you have and intend to have. Give thanks for what you ask for as if it has already happened. If you do not complete the delivery by giving thanks, then you stay in the asking and wanting mode, which is akin to repeatedly sending out your order without receiving the delivery.

Mercury stays in a sign about three weeks, except during its retrograde time, which is explained later in this chapter.

VENUS

The next planet out from the Sun is Venus, signifying *yin feminine* energy such as *romance* and *beauty*. *Female* energy is *magnetic* and acts to *attract* what you desire. Men and women both have Venus energy within them. Everyone carries both male and *female* energy, but one is dominant. Regardless of your sexual orientation, a gender with which you identify dominates your preference.

Venus represents *material* and *social values.* What *value* do you put on the things you desire or have? The *value* includes how much you appreciate them by how well you give care to them. Do you *value* relationships? What *value* do you put on each of your relationships? What do you hold *valuable* in relationship? A day with *harmonic* alignments from the Moon to Venus shown in the daily calendar is usually a good time to participate in social engagements. How to determine such days is discussed in Chapter 6.

For women, Venus is how you relate to being *female* and how you express your *femininity*. For men, where the sign Venus is found in your natal chart represents the kind of *female* you are *attracted* to, especially as a mate.

Venus is connected to the *second chakra*, which governs *sexual* energy. Venus stays in a sign about four weeks, except when it is retrograde, which is explained later in this chapter.

MARS

After the Earth, *yang* Mars is the next planet out from the Sun. Mars signifies the *dynamic male energy* of personal *power*. Mars *fires* you up and *motivates* you to take *action*. It *energizes* you to *act* with courage and confidence. Getting up in the morning and confidently "seizing the day" can be an act of assertiveness.

The *force* of Mars has appropriate and inappropriate applications. It is appropriate to be *forcibly* aggressive in combating threats and violations to anyone's life, liberty, or reasonable pursuit of happiness. It is inappropriate when it disregards those core tenets.

Mars influence can lead one to *initiate* doing one's best. In a *man's* chart, Mars shows his *yang force* of *masculinity* as *he* exerts *his* self-image as a *male*. If *he* is confident of his *masculinity*, *he* does not take anything personally because *he* does not have to prove anything. For a woman, the sign of Mars in her chart represents the kind of *male energy* she is attracted to.

Mars is connected to the *third chakra*. When you feel fear, it is in the *third chakra* at your solar plexus, where it weakens your personal *power*. Mars stays in a sign about six weeks when direct.

JUPITER

Past Mars the next planet out from the Sun is Jupiter, the planet of your *supraconscious mind*. After the Sun, it is the largest planet in the solar system, larger than all the other planets combined. Jupiter's energy is *expansive*. You experience this quality when you *expand* your horizons through travel, or *broaden* your mind through study, or gain understanding of life's laws (human and divine), thereby *increasing* your wisdom.

Jupiter is associated with *symbols* both in your waking and dream life.

Sometimes these *symbols* show up as *archetypes* showing you the truth of a relationship or situation. A jovial Jupiter offers its *optimism* in assisting you to strive toward fulfillment of your aspirations, affirmations, and intentions.

Jupiter is noted for its Red Spot, a massive storm on its surface larger than several Earths, like a hurricane. The Red Spot actually reversed its circular motion. Picture the motion of the water going down the bathtub drain. That motion reversed for the Red Spot, meaning that Jupiter's magnetic field shifted from pole to pole. The South Pole became the North Pole and the North Pole became the South Pole magnetically.

Jupiter stays in a sign for about a year. It is connected to the fifth chakra.

SATURN

Saturn is the next planet past Jupiter and the last of the visible planets. Saturn in your chart has to do with maturity cycles. Psychology books mention the personality development cycles of 7, 14, 21, and 28 years. Astrology describes the same development *patterns* at about the same intervals. These natural maturation periods are called passages that you experience as times of transition to your next developmental period.

At 29-30 years of age you go through your first Saturn return—when it returns to its position at the time of your birth. You experience major life changes of jobs, marriage, divorce, having a child, or going back to school. Your second Saturn return repeats again 29-30 years later, around 58-60 years of age, as completion of the second maturation cycle and the beginning of a third development period of about another 29 years.

In the first cycle of Saturn you are maturing and completing your life of 29-30 years. Frequently people ask, "What am I going to be when I grow up?" From 30 to 60 you are being what you became as you were "growing up" in the previous cycle. A new Saturn cycle then begins. The third Saturn cycle from about 60 to 90 years is the senior cycle of your life. A major question during this cycle is what do you desire to experience in life now that you have the *time* to leave behind your legacy to the planet and the future generations? Within each 29-year cycle is a subdominant theme that cycles about every 7½ years.

The 29-year Saturn cycle is almost identical to the New Moon cycle of 30 days. The Lunar cycle is also made up of subdominant periods of 7½ days that describe the phases of the Moon.

If you were born with Saturn around 3 o'clock in your birth chart, about seven years later it will have moved up to the top of your chart at around 12 o'clock. Fourteen years after your birth it will have moved to around 9 o'clock in your chart. Twenty-one years later, Saturn will have moved to around 6 o'clock. Then, around 29 years of age, it will have traveled back to the same position around 3 o' clock when you were born. Saturn then starts a second cycle. All of the planets eventually cycle back in a three-dimensional spiral to the same position in the sign they were in at your birth.

Since Saturn is associated with *time* and *timing*, it includes *coincidences* and being in *synchronicity*. Being in *synchronicity* means results match your efforts with ease, similar to changing gears smoothly in a vehicle. *Coincidence* means events happen in right *timing* and place, as if you deliberately arranged or planned them. *Coincidences* follow the laws "as above, so below" and "as within, so without."

The rings of Saturn represent the karmic idea of what goes around comes around. Saturn is connected to the *seventh chakra*. It stays in a sign about 2½ years.

TRANSPERSONAL PLANETS

The three outer invisible planets are called transpersonal planets. They generate a higher energy than the visible planets. They are like electrical transformers that transmit voltages from other parts of the galaxy and solar systems into our solar system. They signify not only personal transitions, but also generational transitions, which others experience in a similar time frame to yours.

URANUS

Uranus is the next planet beyond Saturn. Uranus represents the omniscience (all-knowing) of *Infinite Mind*. It is a higher vibratory octave of mental Mercury, not just Mercury consciousness. You can be conscious without being aware or *awakened*. Uranus is associated with *sudden awakening*, *telepathy* and *insight*, a process involving the *unusual* and *unexpected*.

Uranus is the *non-conformist* living life in a *unique, original*, and *un-*

orthodox manner, sometimes even *revolutionary*. The *non-conformity* of Uranus is symbolized by the fact that it rotates on its axis in an opposite spin compared to the other planets. Also, its poles are horizontal at the equatorial positions and its equator is vertical at the polar positions.

Uranus takes 84 years to go around the zodiac. It stays in a sign for about seven years, which marks each of the *generations*. You will have the same sign for Uranus in your chart as your *generation's* age group. What does each generation do? It tends to rebel against the preceding generations by going to extremes, with the pendulum shifting back and forth. Many of the people born in the 1940s became the "flower children" and rebels of the 1960s.

Uranus is connected to your *throat chakra*

NEPTUNE

The next planet out from the Sun is Neptune. It is a higher vibratory octave of Venus. Neptune is connected with your *unconscious* mind through the *sixth chakra*, sometimes referred to as the "*third eye*." What you *project* out as your *vision* is what you experience as your reality. *Vision* includes the qualities of *imagination, inspiration*, and *Divine Guidance*.

Neptune is associated with the *clarity* of the *unconscious*. Your first *impressions* in your feelings—not the mind's judgments—are part of the *unconscious*. The *inner senses* are your advance feelers acting as *guidance* telling you what is coming externally beyond what your conscious mind perceives.

PLUTO

The outermost planet from the Sun is Pluto. On a solar system map you would notice that Pluto's orbit is not a circle, but is unusually elliptical for a planet. You would also notice that Pluto crosses inside the orbit of Neptune, actually making Neptune the outermost planet for a while. Pluto is the only planet that crosses the orbit of another planet. It does so for about 20 years before crossing back over Neptune's orbit, again becoming the outermost planet of the solar system.

Pluto's orbit moves inside Neptune's once approximately every 240 years. The last time it did this was from 1979 to 1999. During the time Pluto crosses in and out of Neptune's orbit it takes about 12 years to go through a sign because it is actually closer to the Sun than Neptune, which speeds up its orbit around the Sun. Normally it takes about 30 years for Pluto to go through a sign. Pluto's shorter travel through a sign means that it does not activate the energy in that sign for as long as it does during its other signs. This has major implications for Pluto's influence in a sign.

Pluto is associated with the *subconscious* mind. Pluto is the higher vibratory octave of Mars's force as *transformative power*. Think of the constant force (Mars) of water carving out the grandeur of the Grand Canyon with a *power* (Pluto) that *transforms* the dirt and rocks of the Earth.

Pluto also represents the *metamorphosis* and *transmutation* of form, such as the caterpillar spinning a cocoon as a chrysalis to *emerge* as a butterfly, or the tadpole that *morphs* into a frog. Another process of Pluto is the cycle of *death* and *rebirth. Decay, disintegration, fertilization, gestation*, and *regeneration recycle* the Earth's matter, such as leaves and wood, into soil for *renewal* as plants and trees.

Pluto has a reputation for requiring you to look at what you are externally attached to for *power* instead of your inner connection to *Power*. At times it strips you of your control over something or someone from which you derived *power*. You have to surrender being "in the Earth." You then can be *transformed, reborn*, and *regenerated* like the caterpillar in the cocoon *metamorphosing* into the dimensional shift of being a butterfly, flying beyond your previous attachment to inauthentic *power*.

Pluto also refers to the process of manifestation through the *power* of your desires. The seed of a desire is planted in your *subconscious* to *incubate* until favorable conditions activate the life force in the seed's embryo, giving *birth* to its potential.

The four types of mind you express through the planets are:
Mercury = consciousness
Jupiter = supraconscious
Neptune = unconscious
Pluto = subconscious

* * *

Retrograde

Retrograde planets appear to travel back over territory in the zodiac they have recently passed through. There are three places in the *Celestial Guide®* that tell you when and for how long a planet goes retrograde. The first place is in the front of the *Celestial Guide®* on the page titled "Planetary Motions." The second place is in the back of the *Celestial Guide®* in the planetary tables. A planet is direct until you see the symbol "R" in the column for the planet in the planetary tables. Read down the columns and look for the retrograde symbol, which begins shading the column. Then follow the shaded area through all the days the planet is retrograde until you see the "D" symbol for direct motion.

The third place is in the daily *Celestial Guide®* pages. A planet is direct until you see its glyph followed by the symbol "SR" (stationary going retrograde) followed by the time it appears to become stationary. The planet remains retrograde until you come to the date where it is listed with its glyph followed by "SD" (stationary going direct) followed by the exact time it again appears to become stationary.

A planet's retrograde cycle gives you a second chance to claim a gift or learn a lesson. You have a third opportunity to build on the gift of a planet's first and second activation when it goes direct after being retrograde. If you have not cleaned up your act during the first or second activation, the third time can be quite a blunt lesson. By the third time an unpleasant experience is meant to get your attention, usually through pain, so that you can learn the lesson. Something is up for you to heal and correct.

The ego will usually respond with: "If he (or she) had only acted differently, or said something differently, I would not be in this situation," or, "You made me angry." No one makes you angry. Getting angry is a choice. By making excuses or projecting the blame onto situations or others, you claim that you are a victim—that is how you give your power away, and how you avoid learning the lesson or healing the wound. It is more useful to say, "What is this experience mirroring to me? What is this opportunity as a lesson meant for me to learn and heal?" (I am not suggesting that abuse or violence is justified just so you can learn a lesson. Abuse and violence are never to be condoned.)

When a planet goes retrograde and then direct, it acts like the ocean tide. A planet's maximum high tide occurs at the time it changes from direct to retrograde. It is at maximum low tide at the time it changes from retrograde motion to going direct. The energy shift involves a time period of days, prior to and after the time of change. Beginning with Mercury, for each planet out from the Sun, you add one day before and one day after the date of the directional change to calculate the period of influence of the Planet.

For instance, starting with Mercury you add one day for the influence. If Mercury is going retrograde or direct then you look for 1 day before and after its exact retrograde day for the period of the directional shift. For Venus, add 2 days before and after the time of the directional shift. Add 3 days for Mars. Jupiter gets 4 days. For Saturn add 5 days. Add 6 days for Uranus. Because Pluto and Neptune's orbits cross each other, give each of them 7 days before and after the date of their directional change.

You will notice in the *Celestial Guide®* that Mercury is the only planet with its own explanation of retrograde motion. Mercury is the most important planet to track retrograde motion. During Mercury retrograde, pay special attention to details, specifics, and small items. The only time I have ever locked myself out of both my house and my car was during two different retrograde periods. If you start something brand new from the idea stage by grounding it during Mercury retrograde you will most likely be with the situation no longer than through the next Mercury retrograde period, which is three months later.

For example if you make an appointment to rent or buy a house, apply for a job, or start a relationship during Mercury retrograde, you will most likely not be in that house, at that job, or in that relationship within three months. If you look at the house, think about applying for a job, or just hear about or see someone you are interested in starting a relationship with during Mercury retrograde, but do not act on the idea until after Mercury is direct, then the retrograde influence does not apply.

If you apply for a job before Mercury goes retrograde and take it while it is retrograde, you are not under the retrograde influence because you initiated the job application before the retrograde period. What you initiate as an action grounds the action. The rule to apply is: grounding an action includes making an appointment, signing a contract, or putting money out for a purchase, even a down payment.

I had a client in Hawaii who hired a contractor to build her house during Mercury retrograde. The contractor frequently ordered either too much or too little materials. In Hawaii when you order lumber and materials from the mainland you cannot just take it back to the store for a refund or an exchange. If you order too much you are stuck with the order. If you do not order enough you not only have to wait until the materials are loaded on the barge but also wait for it to arrive from the mainland. Building your house can take much longer as a result of incorrect ordering. I asked her when she hired the contractor. Sure enough, Mercury was retrograde. She fired him during Mercury direct, hired another contractor and had no more delays.

An example I experienced of the close timing for Mercury's retrograde cycle happened two hours before it went out of retrograde. I had a roommate move out during Mercury retrograde. I needed another roommate to move in so that I could cover the rent. A person showed up two hours before Mercury went direct who wanted the room and who put down the money right then. She moved out to be with a partner three months later during the next Mercury retrograde cycle.

When Mercury retrogrades through its ruling signs of Gemini and Virgo, its retrograde energy is the strongest for applying the positive qualities of those signs.

Tracking and Learning Rulership Planets

Every planet has two "home" signs in which its full power is most easily expressed, except for the Sun and Moon, which each have only one sign. When a planet is in its home sign, it is said to rule that sign. The planet's full power becomes manifested through the themes of its ruling sign(s). You can actually invoke these themes and work with them. They will work for you even if you do not invoke them; however, you will have valuable information available to you by using the *Celestial Guide*® to discover when the planets are in their ruling signs.

Note the day a planet moves into its home sign and track its influence while it is there. Notice events and relationships that signify the planet's strength in its ruling sign. You can use the New Moon meditations in Chapter 7 to strengthen your alignment to a transiting planet while it is in its ruling sign. For example, when Venus is in Taurus you can align yourself with its power while it is there by saying daily the meditation for the New Moon in Taurus. When Mercury is in Gemini you can align yourself with its power while it is there by saying the meditation for the New Moon in Gemini.

To assist you in associating a planet with its home sign(s) of rulership,

I recommend creating a diagram. Draw a circle and then place the signs around the outside edge as you see them on the page of Planetary Motions. Write out the name of the sign just outside the circle. Then put the name of the ruling planet on the inside of the circle next to the sign, so that you begin to associate signs with their ruling planets. On the inside, where you have written the name for the ruling planet, draw the glyph for that planet. Once you know the ruling planet(s) for each sign, you can easily see the compliant sign of each planet, which is the sign directly opposite on the circle.

Once you plot the planets on the circle you can see something interesting about the planetary patterns. You can see Mars ruling Aries between 8 and 9 o'clock and Venus, opposite Mars, ruling Libra between 2 and 3 o'clock. The symbols for male and female energy are opposite each other, just as in life. The ruling sign of masculine Mars is Aries. The opposite sign of Libra is the ruling sign of feminine Venus. They either attract or repel each other depending on who the male and female energy is in life.

The Moon's ruling sign from 6 to 5 o'clock is Cancer, representing the maternal, mother. Opposite Cancer, at 12 to 11 o'clock, is the sign of Capricorn, which is ruled by Saturn, representing the paternal, father.

On the pages of the "Signs of the Zodiac" section, you may want to write out the name and/or glyph of the ruling planet to the right of the name and glyph for the sign. Also, on the pages of the "Planets" section you can note the name and/or glyph of the signs that the planet rules beside the name and glyph for the planet.

Chapter 4 will go into greater detail about the meaning of the signs.

[2] Caroline Myss's book, *The Anatomy of the Spirit,* is an excellent resource for in-depth information about the qualities and issues of the chakras.

Chapter 4

SIGNS

You will notice that the signs go in a counter-clockwise direction on the zodiacal wheel shown in the Planetary Motion chart. Remember that the signs are in a stationary position when you look out at the heavens at night. They do not move. It is the earth's rotation on its axis that makes the signs appear to be moving at a rate of 30 degrees every two hours. Every two hours a new sign is rising at the eastern horizon. All of the signs appear to rise past the 9 o'clock position on the zodiacal circle every 24-hour period because the Earth is rotating counter-clockwise on its axis.

Your birth time tells astrologers where the planets are placed in your chart. If you were born at noon you would have the Sun near the top of your chart at 12 o'clock. If you were born at sunset, the Sun would be near the 3 o'clock position in your chart, where the sky and ground meet on the horizon. The starting point of everyone's chart is always at 9 o'clock, where your Rising sign is located. The Rising sign influences the first section of the circle, which is called the first house. Houses divide the circle of your chart like spokes of a wheel. The 12 houses go counter-clockwise around the circle just like the 12 signs. I will be discussing houses in more detail in Chapter 5.

The signs tell you how a particular planet is going to express itself throughout your life. The signs have dual expressions to their traits. I refer to the two categories as assets and liabilities. They are identifiable patterns specific to how the planets' energy can be expressed on Earth in your birth chart. You can see what opportunities and lessons each planet presents by connecting the planet to the sign it was in at your birth.

A genuine reason for knowing a person's sign is to gauge how aligned or misaligned you are to the qualities of that particular sign. You get along well with people of a particular sign because you have embraced the traits of that sign. If you have not harmonized with the traits of a particular sign, people of that sign will bother or irritate you. You may find yourself judging or reacting to people of that sign. What is it about the person that disturbs you? When you embrace the traits of a particular sign that bothered you, you will no longer have an issue with people of that sign.

I noticed that being around some Leos tended to challenge me. Leo is the sign of authority. Once I identified that I had issues with authority figures and healed my rebellious pattern, I discovered Leos were no longer an issue for me.

The most important connection to make for the planets in your natal chart is what sign the planets are in. The next most important connection to know is the element of the signs. The signs are divided into four elements. The elements follow the same order as the signs around the wheel beginning with fire, earth, air, and water. They are repeated two more times around the zodiac. On the outside wheel of the zodiac, either on your chart or on the "Planetary Motions" page, you can mark the element for each sign, using an abbreviation for each element: fire (f), earth (e), air (a), and water (w). Start with Aries as a fire sign, then Taurus as earth, Gemini as air, and Cancer as water. Repeat the order for the remaining eight signs. Your wheel should correspond to the following chart:

Fire	**Earth**	**Air**	**Water**
Aries	Taurus	Gemini	Cancer
Leo	Virgo	Libra	Scorpio
Sagittarius	Capricorn	Aquarius	Pisces

Fire signs are associated with individuality, creativity, and e-motions—energy in motion. Earth signs are associated with being physical and grounded in the world of materiality. Air signs are mental, associated with communication and relatedness through your relationships such as siblings, partners, and friends. Water signs are associated with your feelings and sensitivity such as intuitions and connectedness with people, including your family.

The next step in understanding the four elements is in knowing the three states that express each element. Fire can be categorized by three expressions: your body's heat (Aries), solar fire (Leo), and combustible fire (Sagittarius). The three qualities of earth are the plains (Taurus), caves and valleys (Virgo), and deserts and mountains (Capricorn). Air has the gentle, playful breezes of late spring (Gemini), the balance between high and low pressure systems (Libra), and the extreme of still air, and the stormy air of tornadoes and hurricanes (Aquarius). Water can exist in the three states of liquid (Cancer), solid ice (Scorpio), and vapor (Pisces).

Love is the primary emotion of fire. Love expresses as will (Leo), joy (Sagittarius), and strength (Aries). Water can be represented by the water cycle of the earth. The journey of water vapor or clouds (Pisces) becomes liquid as rain and snow in the mountains, melting as water in the brooks, creeks, and streams (Cancer). They flow into lakes eventually becoming powerful rivers (Scorpio) that flow into the oceans (Pisces) to rise again as vapor to form rain that begins the journey again as ground water in the mountains. We are all connected to relationships through the air we breathe. As infants we begin to be aware of our neighbors, often as brothers and sisters (Gemini), developing social skills. We eventually have the opportunity to practice those social skills by becoming involved with a partner (Libra). We join with groups and community in yet a larger social network (Aquarius).With earth we make the most of our resources (Taurus) by acquiring the skills to be of service (Virgo) in our job or profession (Capricorn).

The more planets you have in an element in your natal chart the more that element is emphasized in your life. If you do not have any planets in an element it can mean one of two things. You have either mastered that element in other lifetimes and have chosen to only work with the remaining elements, or you have chosen to make it glaringly apparent that you need to work with the missing element, especially through accessing the ruling planets of that missing element. For instance, if you have no planets in earth signs (Taurus, Virgo Capricorn), then the signs' ruling planets (Venus, Mercury, and Saturn) will be especially important for you to be aware of in your chart when they are activated by the planetary cycles.

The next most important connection to make after the elements of your planets is the mode of your planets. The three modes are cardinal, fixed, and mutable. Each mode repeats three times around the zodiac wheel in the same manner as the elements. Cardinal signs initiate the beginning of the seasons, which are also the four directions. The fixed signs are the second sign of each season; they fix the season. Mutable signs are the third sign of each season and represent the transition from one season to the next.

Think of the cardinal mode as referring to starting a business. The fixed mode would refer to the perseverance necessary for at least a year to sustain your business. The mutable mode would be the diversity of products and services you could offer after you have established your business.

Another way to look at the modes is that cardinal would be the motivation to go to college. The fixed mode would be your determination to stay in college to get your degree. The mutable mode refers to what you are going to do with your degree after you graduate—how you adapt and how flexible you are in finding a job. For example, if your degree is in music your choices include being a performer, a teacher, a composer, or music therapist.

The beginning of each season is indicated by the seasonal signs at the ends of the vertical and horizontal lines dividing the zodiacal circle in the "Planetary Motion" chart. The vertical line or axis in your chart from 12 o'clock to 6 o'clock stands for "as above so below." As the boundary between the earth and sky, the horizontal line or axis from 9 o'clock to 3 o'clock stands for "as within so without."

There are three signs per season making up what is called a quadrant. The first sign of spring is Aries at 9 o'clock. Go around the circle 90° counter-clockwise to the bottom at 6 o'clock. You find the sign of Cancer, the first sign of summer beginning the second quadrant. Another 90° takes you to 3 o'clock on the circle. You will find the sign of Libra, the first sign of autumn beginning the third quadrant. Go around another 90° to the top at 12 o'clock. You will find the sign of Capricorn, the first sign of winter beginning the fourth quadrant.

Aries is a cardinal sign beginning with the spring equinox at the left end of the horizontal line dividing the circle. The opposite sign of Libra is a cardinal sign beginning with the autumnal equinox at the right end of the horizontal line dividing the circle. Cancer is a cardinal sign beginning with the summer solstice at the bottom of the vertical line dividing the circle. The opposite sign of Cancer is Capricorn, which is a cardinal sign beginning with the winter solstice at the top of the vertical line dividing the circle. Leo is a fixed sign of the second month of summer and the hottest. The opposite sign of Aquarius is a fixed sign of the second month of winter and the coldest. The fixed sign of Taurus is the second month of spring when flowers and blossoms are in full bloom. The opposite fixed sign of Scorpio is the second month of autumn when fall colors have passed with the frost in most places.

Mutable signs are shifting from the current season as they transition to the next one. The two dual signs of the zodiac, Gemini and Pisces, are mutable signs. They are dual signs because Gemini is depicted by the figure of twins standing next to each other and Pisces is depicted as two fish swimming in opposite directions. Gemini is the third sign of spring, leading into summer. The opposite sign of Gemini is Sagittarius, the third sign of autumn, leading into winter. Virgo is the third sign of summer, leading into autumn. The opposite sign of Pisces is the third sign of winter, leading into spring.

Once you take the initiative of a cardinal sign then you next have the inertia of a fixed sign. Fixed signs are the most determined and persevering of the signs. The Law of Inertia applies to the fixed signs. A lot of energy may be necessary to get a fixed sign moving, but once they are in motion a lot of energy may be necessary to change their direction or stop them. Each fixed sign is followed by a mutable sign that represents adaptability and flexibility. This sequence is repeated three more times around the zodiac, beginning with a different element each time.

On the outside wheel of the zodiac either on your chart or the "Planetary Motions" page you can mark the three modes on the signs. Cardinal signs are always opposite each other on the wheel, as are the fixed and mutable signs. You can use an abbreviation for each mode: cardinal (c), fixed (f), and mutable (m).

Start with Aries as a cardinal sign, then Taurus as a fixed sign, followed by Gemini as a mutable sign. Then repeat the order of the modes for the remaining eight signs. Your wheel should be marked corresponding to the following order:

Cardinal	**Fixed**	**Mutable**
Aries	Taurus	Gemini
Cancer	Leo	Virgo
Libra	Scorpio	Sagittarius
Capricorn	Aquarius	Pisces

You may wish to create a chart with the elements and modes for each sign.

A planet in a sign emphasizes that sign's assets (strengths) and liabilities (weaknesses) more than those signs in which you have no planets in your natal chart. The more planets you have in a sign the more its traits will be emphasized in your life. Your Rising Sign, discussed in more detail later in this chapter, is as important a consideration as having a planet in a sign.

Another way to understand your chart is being aware that each of the signs has a plus or minus charge. Beginning with the plus charge of Aries, the charges alternate around the zodiacal wheel as plus, then minus, then plus and so on. Rating your planets by the plus or minus charge corresponding to the sign they were in at your birth and then adding up the pluses and minuses will give you an overall rating for your masculine and feminine energies. Remember that masculine energies (+) are dynamic and outgoing while feminine energies (–) are receptive and inward. The Sun is androgynous but takes on the plus or minus polarity of whatever sign it shines through.

Description of the Signs

Before the signs are discussed in greater detail a few reminders are helpful in using the following information. As you read the description of each sign, remember that each of us has both the assets and the liabilities of all 12 signs within us. The 12 signs are a wheel, a wheel that we are all a part of, and that we all participate in expressing. Therefore, the signs are part of us and not just a trait or personality profile that excludes the qualities and traits of the other signs.

A planet does not cause our human experience, but the rays of Light reflected from the planet shine into the traits of the sign's assets and the solutions for its potential liabilities can be revealed. These assets and liabilities are specifically addressed by the meanings of the ruling, exalted, compliant, and receptive planets for each sign. By being compliant or receptive to a planet's specific energy in each sign, it provides the solution to the liability of its sign, and we can turn the liability into an asset. A compliant planet offers its energy to us so that any misapplication of the sign's energy can be corrected and realigned with the compliant planet's qualities. A receptive planet offers its energy to us so that any misapplication of the sign's energy can be corrected and realigned with the receptive planet's qualities.

Any energy pattern out of alignment with the assets of a sign will be activated into our experience to be healed or mastered. In whatever sign we have planets, we can draw strength from the planets to compensate for the potential liabilities (weaknesses) of the sign.

In the descriptions below, the keywords for each sign are in italics. Delineating the keywords this way is meant to clear up ambiguous meanings for the signs when keywords are used for more than one sign in astrological literature. Also included for each sign is one meaning of its compliant, receptive, ruling, and exalted planet.

ARIES

Aries is a cardinal fire sign of *impulse* that can be equated with *assertiveness* and *initiative*. *Impulses propel actions* toward new growth as the *impulse* of the seed *impels* it toward the Earth's surface. Aries includes *competition* by being *competitive* with our self to *be* and *do* more than our last *effort*. Aries is also where we have the *motivation* that *impels* new directions in our life that may require *courage*, a trait of *warriors*, *pioneers* and *leaders*.

The liabilities of Aries are *impatience, selfishness, discouragement, unprovoked anger, hatred* of yourself that *targets hating* others, and the *inhibition* to *be assertive* and *standing up* for yourself. When we block an authentic *impulse,* our *initiative* and *motivation* become stifled and clogged with *resistance*. *Selfish impulsiveness* is usually the *reactionary* behavior associated with a quick to *trigger temper*—quick to *anger*. A *combative, angry* person is usually being *macho* and often *ruthless.*

Venus, as the compliant planet, offers harmony, peace, and considerate treatment of others instead of unprovoked *anger*, *hatred, temper tantrums*, and *willful selfishness*.

When we are receptive to Saturn's qualities, it offers patience to *impatience.* Saturn supports the right timing of the *impulse* for a new direction. That *impulse* also *encourages* so that we are not *inhibited* from taking the *initiative*.

Mars as the ruler of Aries fires us up to initiate our maximum *effort* in our *actions* with *courage* and *confidence*, especially when we have become *discouraged*.

The most important consideration for Aries energy is the *motivation* behind our *actions*. When *motivation* is *tempered* with Divine *Impulse,* represented by the exalted Sun here, we *stand up* with the *strength* of a *courageous warrior* for the Light in all our *actions*.

TAURUS

The fixed earth sign of Taurus includes how we *earn money* that is *exchanged* for *goods* and *products* through *valuing* our *talents, gifts*, and *abilities*. What we *value materially* is shown by the *quality* of what we *buy* to *own* and *possess* as well as how much we are willing to *pay* for *products* and *goods*. Like the *farmer* who shows what crops he/she *values* by what is *cultivated,* our *value* is also shown by what we *cultivate* to be *worthy* of our *talents, gifts*, and *abilities*.

Valuing our *talents, gifts*, and *abilities* involves our *self-worth* and *self-esteem*. Our *self-worth builds* our *self-esteem*. The greater our *self-worth* the greater our *self-esteem.*

The Law of *Receiving* and *Giving* states that the more we *receive,* the more *resources* we have to *give,* which continues the cycle. *Material* imbalances are the result of either *taking* more than we gi*ve* or *giving* more than we *received* to *compensate* for low *self-esteem*. What happens to a bank *account* when we withdraw more than we deposit? Eventually we would go into the *poverty* of *material* and energetic debt. By saying that it is better to *give* than to *receive* we set ourselves up to be in this position. It is as important to *receive* as it is to *give*.

A client who said she shoplifted from big corporate stores exemplified one liability of Taurus. She added, "Who's watching? Nobody." I reminded her that her witness self is like a video camera with audio that records all her actions. It holds the record of her karma to be dispensed in her cycles. Since Taurus is the sign of *material values*, she *values taking* what she can *get* rather than *paying* for the *things* she *acquires*. In this case her *material values* then set up a resonance in her second chakra (Venus rules Taurus) to be *taken* from.

Give equal importance to both *giving* and *receiving* to maintain a balanced *account* both *materially* and energetically. What we do with what we *have* determines its *valu*e to us. By being *possessive, hoarding*, or *stingy* we attract *losing* by trying to grab what we can *get*. In *greedily* holding on to what we *have* we do not *value sharing*. We are *claiming* that we do not *have* enough to be *materially* secure no matter what we *have*.

Taurus, a compliant sign for Mars, can motivate us to *persevere* in *cultivating* and *building* our *talents* and *gifts*, thereby strengthening our *self-worth* and *self-esteem.*

Taurus is also a compliant sign for Pluto, the planet of shared power.

When we *value* fair *acquisition* of *material resources* over *getting, taking,* and *stealing,* we increase our *wealth* by the Law of *Receiving* and *Giving,* which states that whatever we *value* and appreciate attracts more of the same.

Taurus is a receptive sign for Uranus, the planet of change. By being receptive to change we can avoid being *stubborn* about changing when our *attachment* to something prevents new growth, such as holding on to a toxic job just for *financial* security when changing jobs would be *valuing* our *talents.* Taurus, being a fixed Earth sign, can be grounded in *perseverance* and *endurance* without being too *stubbornly* fixed when the necessity to change arises.

Venus, the ruling planet for Taurus, reminds us that we attract more prosperity through the Law of Attraction when we value and appreciate what we have.

The maternal fertile Moon is exalted in Taurus because as *stewards,* we nurture the *productivity* of Mother-Earth, which *gives* everything *materially* to humanity, by *valuing* and *conserving* the *resources* of our planet.

GEMINI

Gemini is the mutable air sign of l*earning* and communicating *information* and *knowledge.* Every *idea* we *learn* and every *statement* we make represents our *intelligence* or *ignorance* (not necessarily *stupidity). Intelligent* communication and *intelligent comprehension* is involved with and necessary for *correct teaching* and *learning.*

The *twins* of Gemini are our *perception* and *interpretation* of what we *perceive. Perception* is based on another set of *twins* -- what we *look* at and *hear.* Our *interpretation* is also based on a set of twins -- how well we *see* what we *look* at and how well we *listen* to what we *hear* in our *immediate environment,* based on what our *attention* is on. For example, you *perceived* correctly that two people are having an intense *dialogue.* Your second step of *interpretation* may or may not be *correct,* depending on how accurately you *interpret* what you *perceive.* The two people may not be angry with each other, or in a hurry, but just excited about what they are communicating about.

We *interpret correctly* or *incorrectly* what we *perceive,* which then becomes our *conclusion.* If our *perception* is *correct,* then we have a chance that our *interpretation* will be *correct*. However, we may *perceive correctly* but then *misinterpret* what we *perceive* because of our *preconceptions* from the *memory* of past experiences. An example is the courtroom drama where five people were at the scene of a hit-and-run accident. Their *stories* amounted to five different *versions* of what happened. How could we have five different *versions* of what happened? *Perception* and *interpretation*. One person's *attention* may be on the facial expressions of the drivers. Another's *attention* may be on the make of the cars involved. A third may *see* a broader picture encompassing the intersection where the accident took place and the placement of other *vehicles* in the scene. A male witness may assume that the woman *driver* must be at fault if he has an *attitude* about women drivers. And so on. The possibilities are limited only by the number of witnesses.

You may have *heard* that people tend to *hear* what they want to *hear* and *see* what they want to *see*, which is selective *perception* and selective *interpretation*. What we *think* of as important *data* will be the focus of our *attention* for any *event*, including a *car* accident. We *disregard data* we do not *perceive* as important even though other *data* is within our field of *perception*. Our *nervous system* will also invalidate *data* that conflicts with our *belief* system. It tunes out contrary *data* by filtering out *information* it labels as "*spam*" before it gets to our *brain*.

Gemini also refers to our *story* about how we *perceive* life through our *beliefs, attitudes* and *opinions*. Our *story* then becomes our 'internal *dialogue*' that constantly *reminds* us of the *script* we have *written* for our self about how life is.

Every *story* has two sides beyond the *true* and *false* sides that we have been *taught* always exist. If I am *talking* to another I am *transmitting* my *story* as one side to another (the other side) who has to make *sense* of it to *receive* my communication. A clear *transmitter* and an *attentive receiver* are necessary for communication to occur.

One liability of Gemini refers to people being *superficial* in their *conversations* and *thinking* they *know* more than they actually do *know*. They may also be *mistaken* that their '*facts*' and *figures* are *correct*. They may be either consciously *dishonest* to cover up a *lie* or *dishonest* as the result of being *superficial* with their *learning,* leading to *false conclusions* and *opinions*. All *excuses* are attempts to make what is *false true* by *justifying* and *rationalizing misperceptions* and *false conclusions*. By making *excuses, rationalizations*, and *justifications* we deny *correction* of our *mistakes* and remain in *ignorance*

Our *conclusions* and *ideas* contribute to our *rational* or *irrational mind*, depending on the *correctness* of our *learning. Irrational thinking* and *talking* stem from *incorrect* and *false learning*. If we *objectively question* all that we have been *taught*, then our *knowledge* can be only what is *correct* and *true*.

Stupidity is one of the liability traits of Gemini where even *common knowledge* or social rules of appropriate communication can be *ignored*. Having an *attitude* can reflect the potential crassness of Gemini energy. Many politicians and *talk* show hosts have been *reminded* that *words* reflect *intelligence, ignorance*, or downright *stupidity*. Being politically *correct* or *incorrect* falls under Gemini's domain.

In Gemini the *twin* roles of *question* and *answer* are *emphasized* much like the *true/false tests* we took in *school* that *tested* our *memory*. Our *memory* also functions as our internal *secretary*, *reminding* us of our to-do *list* of activities such as *errands* and making *phone calls*.

Gemini is connected with our *sense of humor, comedy*, and *fun*. *Playing games* is included under Gemini's influence.

Gemini has no exalted planet, being one of the two Mercury-ruled signs where no planet is exalted.

Gemini is a compliant sign for Jupiter, the planet of truth and honesty. When we *communicate* and *teach information* based on being compliant with Jupiter's quality of what is *true*, we *learn* of *true knowledge* rather than the *ignorance* of mere *superficial beliefs, attitudes*, and *opinions* that *interfere* with *knowledge*.

Gemini is a receptive sign for Neptune, the planet of clarity. By being receptive to clear *perception* and *interpretation*, we avoid *misperceptions* and *misinterpretations*. Neptune's quality of clarity avoids *lies* and deliberate *dishonesty* that *interfere* with *communicating honestly*.

Mercury, as the ruling planet for Gemini, offers the *intelligence* of the conscious mind for our *curiosity* and *interest* in *learning* of the *diverse subjects* available to us for *study*.

CANCER

The cardinal water sign of *domestic* Cancer refers to your *home, family*, and *roots*, including your *nation* of *origin*. The *preservation* of your *family* and *nation* are based on Cancerian *traditions* and *conventions*. Your feelings of *safety* and *security* both as a child and an adult *provide* a *protective shell* of *comfort* like the Cancer *crab*. A *protective* mother provides for the *safety* and *caring* of her child. Without a feeling of *safety* and *comfort* for being provided with the basic essentials for *security*—such as water, food, clothing, shelter, and affection a child is likely to feel *rejected, abandoned,* and *insecure*– liabilities of Cancer. Other liabilities here are being overly *protective* or *neglectful* of the *needs* of others, especially *family* members who are dependent on us, including children and pets.

Track the Moon's passage through its ruling sign of Cancer. Every 28 days the Moon is in the water sign of Cancer, which brings out the strongest qualities of the Moon. Your feelings about *home* and *security* can be stimulated when the Moon is transiting Cancer. You may do chores around your *home* that add to your feeling of *comfort* and *security*. Being around people who you call *family* will be important

Cancer is a receptive sign for Mars. Its energy *supports* the growth of developing *offspring* with *safety* and the fierce *protectiveness* of a mother bear.

Cancer is a compliant sign for Saturn because, like the *crab's shell*, it sets limits. If we are compliant to Saturn's limits, then we avoid too much reliance on the status quo of *traditions* and *conventions* that may stifle growth and development. Too much *mothering* and *protection* can "drown" a child if limits are not set on the *nurturing* of the *foundation* of one's personality, which is vital for *supporting* a child's *security* and growth.

The Moon rules Cancer, offering *mothering* for our *security, support*, and *comfort* in our *family* and *home.*

Jupiter, the planet of the future and mores, is exalted in Cancer by *preserving* the sacred *traditions* and *conventions* of the *heritage* of each *family, culture, race*, and *nation* for the *nurturing* of future generations

LEO

In the fixed fire sign of Leo your *will* for *self-expression* of your *individuality* is through your *creativity* and *loved ones*, including *children.* You also *express* yourself through *re-creation*, which includes *love affairs, amusements* and *entertainment*.

Leo represents the *stage* of your life on which the asset of your Self *dramatically stars*, like an *actor* (*hero* or *heroine*) without losing her or his core identity. Your Self is naturally *proud* of its *creative expressions* of Spirit through the Divine Will of Love. If you are identified as a liability with the *arrogant* and *pompous will* of *ego*, then it *melodramatically* plays out its role on your *stage* with *humiliating* results. The *conceited ego* is *self-absorbed* with its *grandiose* displays of *self-centeredness* always having to be the *star*.

In Leo you choose to either be *Self-centered* or *ego-centered*, *Self-conscious* or *ego-conscious*. Whatever self you are centered on *will* be the self you are conscious of in your *self-expression*. Everyone is *self-centered*, but what self are they centered on and thereby give consciousness and *expression* to?

The *ego* causes the *melodrama* of pain and suffering in your life. You know people who are involved in the big production of *melodrama* in their lives, sometimes referred to as *drama queens* or *drama kings*. The *ego* is always concerned with getting itself in the *spotlight* for attention, including *boasting* how great and *grandiose* it is.

Leo is a fire sign representing *love* and *fear*—the only two emotions that you can *express* as the source of your life. The *expressions* of *love* have various *creative expressions* of your Self such as joy and enthusiasm. The *expressions* of *fear* have various *miscreated expressions* as ego such as destructive anger and selfishness.

Leo is a compliant sign for Uranus. It expresses the originality of our *individuality* and *creativity* through love without being *ego-centered*, *arrogant,* and *melodramatic*.

Leo is also a compliant sign for Saturn. We can compliantly design our lives through the *expression* of Divine Love as the only *authority* in our lives, rather than living from *fear*.

Leo is a receptive sign for Mercury, the planet of consciousness. We can be *Self-conscious* in our *creation*s by being receptive to the dual expressions of Leo as Unconditional Love and Divine Will. Being receptive to Unconditional Love and Divine Will avoids *miscreation*s, which are *expressions* of an *egotistical* mind.

The Sun rules Leo, shining with Love's generosity and illuminating the world with the bountifulness of Light through our *heart's expression*.

Pluto's power is exalted in Leo, signifying that Love is the only authentic Power there is to create and express who we are.

VIRGO

The mutable earth sign of our *analytical mind,* Virgo, is concerned with *discernmen*t or right *evaluation* of what we *analyze*, especially the *specifics* and *details* of *health* and *work*.

Virgo is concerned with *mental health*, which includes the quality of *discretion* and *objective discernment* in contrast to *subjective judgment* as *prejudice* and *bias.* One of Virgo's assets is the right *discernment* of *objective analysis—analyzing* with *objective criticism,* not *condemning criticism* or *judgment.*

Mental health includes *healing judgments* and *condemning criticisms* from the inner *judge*. We have two reactions in Virgo: to *judge* people and situations or *serve* them with *healing* light. We can *clea*r and *hea*l the *judgment* or continue to point our finger in *condemnation* at who and what we *judge*. We can be an *objective discerning healer* without getting on the 'high horse' of *judgment*.

A *judgment* becomes truth, unexamined for its *prejudice* and *bias*. For instance, you may *judge* someone as living life stupidly or learning a lesson in a 'dumb' way. You *critique* them in a superior *holier-than-thou*-attitude saying, something like, "I would never say that" or "I would never do it that way." You have just assured yourself that another will tell you *judgmentally* that they would not ever say what you said or that another will tell you *judgmentally* that they would not ever do it your way.

"Never" is a charged ultimatum that attracts what we say "never" about. We attract what we resist because we give the issue attention. A client had said that he would never get married, never have a child, and never live in L.A. He has done all three of these ultimatums.

Your *judgments* are imprinted in your energy field, returning to you like salmon returning to the spawning grounds to live out that *judgment*. A *judgment* freeze-frames the *condemning criticism* into your psyche, setting you up to attract it in some way. If someone needles you, bothers you, is being *nit-picky*, or is acting as a '*petty tyrant*', see if you can trace the cause as a *judgment* about a person in your past. You tend to be like what bothers you. If you find yourself in an unpleasant situation, check inside to see if one of your *judgments* has returned to you.

If you have made *condemning criticisms* or *judgments,* they return to you when an activating planet is in Virgo, when a planet activates Virgo planets, or when a planet activates Mercury, which rules Virgo. When you *judge* another, the *judgment* has your energy signature on it and can return to you when any of the above mentioned alignments happen in your natal chart.

Virgo is connected to our physical *health*—where and how we can *improve* our life. The importance of eating *organic food* is included in Virgo's qualities of *unadulterated purity. Organic food* has more *nutrition* and life force than *non-organic foods.* They also do not have the poisonous sprays and *additives* that build up over time. These toxins compromise our immune system and interfere with both communication between DNA nuclei and the function of neurotransmitters by destroying biochemical pathways in the body. Virgo is where we *heal* ourselves, which includes *cleansing* and *purification.*

An asset of Virgo is *service* through helping others *heal* themselves, including their *unhealthy doubt* about such things as *methods, techniques*, and *skills* that would help them become *healthier* or *improve* their *work. Healthy doubt* is *healthy skepticism,* which questions while reaching a final *analysis.*

Virgo is a sign of *employer-employee, student-teacher*, and *healer-client* relationships. See if your *healer, nurse, massage therapist*, or *hairstylist* is a Virgo Sun, Moon, or Rising Sign.

Virgo has no exalted planet, being one of the two Mercury-ruled signs where no planet is exalted.

Virgo is a compliant sign for Jupiter. Jupiter's expansiveness can assist us from getting bogged down in *scrutinizing* the trees in *trivial detail* and *analysis,* thereby failing to see the forest or larger picture.

Virgo is a receptive sign for Venus. By being receptive to the love and peace of Venus and being *dedicated* and *devoted* to *healing,* we avoid *condemning criticism* and *judgment* of others and ourselves.

Virgo is a compliant sign for Neptune. Being compliant to Neptune's guidance in the form of inner senses can help us sort out the various *methods, techniques*, and *tools* of *healing* and *crafts* of our work. The *discernment* of a *healthy* mind is then not too *skeptical* of what is possible.

Mercury, the ruling planet for Virgo, offers the *discernment* of the conscious mind in *service* to our *devotion,* and *devotion* to our *service.*

LIBRA

Libra is a cardinal air sign referring to how we make *decisions*. We make them based on *agreemen*t with our *social values* or *compromising* them just to *please* another in order to be *accepted.* Making a *decision* not only involves *deciding* what *decision* to make without Libra's liability of *procrastination*, but also implementing it in action without being overly concerned with *pleasing* another.

Your Self does not *compromise* in loving another. Your Self does not come down to Earth and lower its quality of love just for *acceptance* or *approval*. If you do, you *compromise* your *social values*. Your Self waits for you to meet the quality of love of your Self.

What is the first relationship you always have and carry with you throughout your lifetime? Yourself. One of the qualities of Libra is *value*—how you *value* your self. Do you *compromise* how you think about your self in *social* relationships? The *balance* is between being *considerate* of your self <u>and</u> others.

Libra knows that every *decision* results in *peace* or *conflict*. The *peacemakers* of Libra include *advisors, counselors, negotiators*, and *mediators* who assist people to have *harmony* in their relationships. They are concerned with *conflict resolution*. Those who *value conflict* will be in *conflict* with *fair* and *just decisions*, including *compromise*s and *litigation*.

A Libra quality is standing up for the *rights* of others in *fair* and *just treatment*. A Libra may also be required to stand up for his or her *rights*, including confronting *double standards*.

Libra includes *joining* in *mutual cooperation* and *consideration* in *marriage* and *partnership*. If each person *appreciates* what the other brings to the *partnership* in equal *value*, then *mutual accord* and *agreement* can prevail in all their *joint decisions*. Their *shared aesthetic values* of *beauty* and *romance* will contribute to their common purpose for being *together* as a *due*t of two musicians.

Libra is a compliant sign for Mars. Mars can motivate us to confidently make our *decisions* without *procrastination*. Mars can also be forceful in standing up for the *rights* of others and ourselves in *fairness* without *compromise*, especially to those valuing *conflict*.

Libra is a receptive sign for the Sun. The Sun shines on all with *equal thoughtfulness*, *consideration*, and *appreciation*. The Sun lends its light in *appreciation* of others, without *compromising* itself by valuing another's *acceptance* or *approval* just to be loved.

Venus, the ruler of Libra, offers us the *choice* to *decide* for *peace* rather than *conflict* with every *decision* and every *agreement* we make.

Saturn, exalted in Libra, reminds us that everyone is *equal* under the *Golden Rule*. Being *treated fairly* is based on our *treatment* of others—an impersonal law that has personal effects echoed by the saying, "What goes around comes around." Saturn always *balances* the *scales* sooner or later.

SCORPIO

The fixed water sign of Scorpio is the domain of shared *empowerment*, including *finances* and *sexuality* in the partnerships of Libra. Partnerships of *passionate* mutual accord have at least four times more *power* together to *manifest* their *desires* than each person has singularly. The *intensity* of your *passion* is your *power* to *manifes*t your *desires.* How well does a couple *manifest* together and what do they *manifest* with their joined *powers*? The results will either be *constructive transformation* or the *destructive shadow* of *self-sabotage*.

Scorpio also includes death and rebirth. When two people marry or partner in Libra what do they *die* to? They *die* (*surrender*) to a certain sense of their singularity—not their individuality. The joint sharing of *taxes, banking, credit cards*, and *inheritance*s factor into their union. If you have at least one planet in Scorpio watch how your finances increase or decrease once you form a partnership legally or by common law. The value of each person's agreement to *surrender* his or her singularity to join with the other will be the telling bottom line.

Any issues of *power* involve the liability side of Scorpio. Struggles of *control* through *manipulation* and *coercion* lead to feelings of *resentment* and the *vindictiveness* of *revenge*.

Scorpio refers to water in *lakes, reservoirs*, and being in the solid *frozen* state of *ice* as well as *stagnant*—not flowing. When we *stuff* our feelings they become *stagnant* or *frozen-like*.

Scorpio is the sign of both the higher *subconscious* of *constructive manifestation* and the lower subconscious of the *destructive shadow side.* The higher *subconscious* includes *forgiveness* and *empowerment* to *mani-*

fest your *constructive desires.* Your lower *subconscious* is the *basement* holding your *stagnated* energy of *grievances* and *wounds* where you have felt *vulnerable*

We *erect armament* and *defenses* around our *intense wounds*, which *disempowers* us. Other people are then able to push our *charged buttons*, which *tunnel* to our unresolved *cauldrons*. We then tend to react *intensely* even to a seemingly mild *offense*, even if none was intended. When they are *thawed* out those feelings are like the proverbial 'straw that broke the camel's back. The cork blows from the *intense pressure.*

The eventual *meltdown* of *defenses* as *armament* makes you *vulnerable* to further *wounding* and *resentments* until through *forgiveness* you are no longer willing to keep paying the price for being hurt. *Forgiveness* means you are no longer willing to allow another's harm to keep you *disempowered.* You can *reclaim* your *power* back from the original *transgression* by transmuting it through *forgiveness.* Sometimes it requires deep *excavation* of the *wounds* in the *secret vaults* of your lower *subconscious* before the *transmutation* of *forgiveness* can begin.

Moon in Scorpio every 28 days has to do with your *subconscious.* People tend to *reveal* their *shadow* side through being *defensive, resentful* and a tendency to hold *grudges* and *grievances.* For those of you doing therapy and healing processes the 2 1/2 days while the Moon is in its receptive sign of Scorpio is when the deepest *wounds* and issues can be triggered because the body no longer *desires* to hold on to the *toxicity* of those *wounds.* For those of you working with the public you may wish to pay special attention to when the Moon is in Scorpio. People's *'buttons'* are more easily pushed and you can get over-exaggerated *eruptions* to comments and curious questions like "When is dinner going to be ready?" "It's not ready! Fix it yourself!" People's *subconscious* stuff can more easily surface.

Scorpio is the domain of your *sub-conscious*—energies that are *subterranean* like *oil, crystals*, and *gold* beneath the surface of the Earth. The lower *subconscious* is your *shadow* side. If your mate, child, or boss is really sensitive and you wish to approach them about an issue with the Moon receptive in Scorpio, check in with your guidance about talking to them. They may already being triggered with their "stuff" and may not be able to be fully present to listen to you.

Scorpio is connected to the *forces* of nature like *earthquakes, volca-*

noes, and *tidal waves*. Watch the news around three days of a New or Full Moon in Scorpio for major *earthquake* and *volcanic* activity. In your psyche the same kind of energy can be released like the cork being blown out of the champagne bottle. People can be a lot more emotional and sensitive as the *shadow* side of human nature can be more easily triggered and expressed.

Scorpio is connected with our *reproductive* as well as our *eliminative* systems. I had a Scorpio friend tell me that he can always tell when the Moon is in the sign of *toilet bowl*. That was his shorthand for his stuff surfacing – time to *eliminate toxic* feelings.

Remember that Scorpio is the transformation of the seed when the warmth of the Sun stimulates it to break open its shell. It then can grow toward the surface of the Earth and sprout forth into the sunlight. Another example is like the chick that has to peck itself out of the egg to the outside. It does not know what is on the other side of the shell, but if it does not peck through the shell, it *dies*. On the other side of the shell is the *unknown* - a whole new world in which to live. The higher *subconscious* of *constructive manifestation* is similar to the process where the egg breaks open in response to the birth of new life or the bud *bursting* open to blossom in sweet fragrance and colorful display.

When the New Moon is in Scorpio you will wish to track its energy for the following four weeks. When the Full Moon is in Scorpio you will wish to track its energy for the following two weeks.

Scorpio is a receptive sign for the Moon. Being receptive to the Moon's water nature allows us to *melt* the *defenses* and *armaments* around our *wounds* so that *suppressed, stagnant feelings* do not shorten our life span. They can then be *eliminated* through *intense excavation* and *forgiveness*, allowing us to live life more *empowered* and better able to *manifest* our *constructive desires*.

Scorpio is a compliant sign for Venus. By *investing* in love, no matter what, we have the *power* through *forgiveness* of *grievances* to overcome feelings of *vindictiveness, retaliation*, and *revenge,* which *disempower* us with their *toxicity*. *Forgiveness* does not mean that what another did to *violate* and *wound* is justified, but that we are no longer willing to be *manipulated* and *controlled* by their *destructive* behavior.

Mars, one of the two rulers of Scorpio, offers its force when you join with another in *passion* to *manifest* your *desires* together.

Pluto, the second ruler of Scorpio, offers its *constructive power* for the transformation and transmutation of what you have *surrendered* to emerge in a rebirth of deeper *power.*

Uranus, the planet of Infinite Mind, is exalted in Scorpio. Whenever we *relinquish* the *desire* to be in *control,* we invoke the *power* of the deeper *mysteries* of the *Great Unknown.* The *unfathomable* and *unknown* of Infinite Mind can then *manifest* in our lives. Everything that happens is unexpected because you cannot expect anything in the *Great Unknown.*

SAGITTARIUS

The mutable fire sign of Sagittarius embodies *understanding* the *meaning* of facts, figures, and knowledge of its opposite sign of Gemini as *wisdom*. Hence the question, "What does it all *mean*?" We *seek* to *understand* the *meaning* of life through *religion, politics, philosophy, psychology, metaphysics,* and *spirituality*. We base our *ethics, principles,* and *morality* on how we *understand* these subjects and make them our *truth*.

Sagittarius is also associated with the *meaning* of *symbols,* including *signs, omens,* and *dream symbols*. I once lived in the Hawaiian Islands. After I had moved back to the mainland, I did a hike with my northern turnaround point at Island Lake in the Wind River Wilderness of Wyoming. When I arrived at the lake, I noticed small rock islands in the nearly-mile-long lake, just like the Hawaiian Islands in the middle of the Pacific Ocean. My southern turnaround point was Rainbow Lake, which was not intentional. Hawaii is noted for its prolific rainbows. I had gotten on the "wrong" trail because grazing sheep obscured the area where the trail forked. My first introduction to this hiking area was about thirty years before this hike when I attended a Rainbow Gathering.

Another example involves a *dream* I had about gambling in a casino with multi-colored neon lights. I took this *dream* literally since I am not a gambler. To test it out I drove ninety miles to a place with casinos. The first casino I walked into had neon lights, not multi-colored lights. So I went to a second casino that had multi-colored lights, but it did not feel right. I went to a third casino that had multi-colored neon lights in the ceiling. The floor had the planets pictured on the carpet. So I found the keno area and played my first keno card which did not win anything. I filled out a second card, then thought I should change my bet with less numbers until I figured out how Keno worked. I filled out a third card with less numbers and won several hundred dollars. But, when I looked at the second card still on my table, I was amazed and disappointed to see that if I had played the extra numbers I would have won several thousand dollars! I had second-guessed myself!

The liabilities of Sagittarius include *closed-mindedness, self-righteousness, hypocrisy,* and *intolerance* (*bigotry*). *Religious fanaticism* is one example of the extreme of these traits. Conversely, an asset of Sagittarius is *open-mindedness* with a sense of *adventure* to *explore* new *horizons* and *vistas.*

The symbol for Sagittarius is a centaur shooting an *arrow* upwards. Our *aspirations* are *arrows* of energy *aimed* at the *mark* of our *intentions* and *affirmations*. We can be *enthusiastic* and *optimistic* toward fulfillment of our *aspirations, affirmations*, and *intentions*.

Sagittarius is a compliant sign for Mercury. By being conscious of *open-mindedness* about what is *truth,* we can avoid being *self-righteous, intolerant,* and *hypocritical* like the *know-it-all.*

Jupiter, the ruling planet for Sagittarius, offers its Truth for our *principles, ethics*, and *moral standards* in our *understanding* of human and Divine *Laws*. Jupiter can expand our *horizons* through *long-distance travel* and *exploration*, *broadening* our *perspective* and *tolerance.*

Neptune, the planet of Vision, is exalted in Sagittarius. We can *understand* with Vision how everything is *unified* in a *holistic synergy* of the *affirmation* of life. We gain *wisdom* in *enjoying* the *adventure* of *ever-expanding horizons* and *ports of call.*

CAPRICORN

The cardinal earth sign of Capricorn is the sign that *governs ambitions* that are carried out in your *business, job*, or *profession*. *Ambition* can include *plans* and *schedules* that *map* out what you are seeking to *accomplish* and *achieve*, which usually require *patience*. *Delays* to your *ambitions* can be caused by *rigidity*, which can then result in *disappointment, pessimism*, and *depression.*

Another asset of Capricorn is having the *practicality* to know what to do and when to do it like an *engineer* or *architect*. The *architect* within you is *designing* and *structuring* your life according to your *purpose*, which involves *patient* and *cautious planning.* How do you *design* a highway, a bridge, or a building? You begin with a "*blueprint*" that *structures* the *project.* You then *organize* and *accomplish* your *plan step by step*, which can be *patterned* after the *Divine Plan* and *Order.* Be *cautious*, however, not to be like the *workaholic* who requires firm *boundaries* so as to not be *driven* by too much to do and not enough *time* to do it!

Capricorn includes the qualities of *accountability, reliability*, and *responsibility*. How *reliable* and how *impeccable* is your *integrity* in regard to your *position* and *status* concerning *government, bosses, supervisors*, and *managers*? *Honor* or *dishonor* follows this assessment. *Dishonor* is what is meant by the saying, "The higher they *climb*, the harder they fall." The higher the *position* the harder the fall when *accountability* is not *responsibly recognized.*

In almost all the charts I have seen in which a person is born with their Moon in Capricorn, they have had some kind of a *struggle* with lack of affection, nurturing, or support from at least one of the parents. Their early life was *difficult* from *burdens* or *responsibilities* not normal for a child growing up. They may have had to take care of the other children because one or both parents were not home much. One of the parents might have been emotionally absent. They had to grow up with an abnormal amount of *stress* and *hardship* and were pushed into a level of *maturity* and nurturing not common to a normal childhood. However, the Moon being in Capricorn did not cause the hardships. To the contrary, by being in compliance with the Moon's qualities, Capricorn was provided additional nurturing and nourishing for them, supporting what *discipline* was required to *accomplish* their *tasks.*

When the Moon travels through Capricorn, which includes *mountains* and *deserts* where little water is found, people generally require more support to get in touch with their feelings than when the Moon is in other signs because of their being *pessimistic, stuck* in a *rut*, and *depressed.*

The Moon is a water planet. In its compliant sign of Capricorn its water has to rise above *obstacles* and *barriers* until it flows around or through them. Once while the Moon was in Capricorn I began my day with a list of about twelve errands to do. By the *time* I had gotten to the fourth errand I was ready to return home, thinking how uncanny were the many *delays* and *obstacles* I had met. I could not go around or through the *obstacles* in my case! My timing was off trying to push ahead with my *ambition* to *accomplish* getting things done. Instead, my push to get things done added to my being *stressed-out* on that day. I really needed to stay home and nurture myself—a Moon quality.

Sometimes *delays* can be a *rerouting* of your opportunities, like following a *detour.* I had an experience like this when the freeway off-ramp was closed to a *road* that I intended to take to a camping place off the beaten *path* for the fall equinox. Since I had left after *work* the Sun was setting before I was near my *destination,* so I found a campground after dusk and drove into it. I recently had a strong, unusual experience with a hawk in the wilderness. When I drove out the next day I saw that the name of the campground was "Black Hawk Campground."

While the Moon is in Capricorn, people can tend to be *late* or *fail* to show up for *appointments* more than usual. The ruling planet Saturn is showing them their need to be more *organized* and less *stressed.*

Capricorn is the compliant sign for the Moon. Water, a quality associated with the Moon, rises *patiently* above *obstacles* and *barriers* until it flows around or through them. Being compliant to the Moon's maternal support assists us in overcoming *struggle, hardship,* and *stress,* which can *burden* us with the *heavy weight* of too much *obligation* and *duty.*

Capricorn is a receptive sign for Jupiter. We can draw on Jupiter's expansive optimism to overcome *disappointment, depression, pessimism,* and being *stuck in a rut* of *futility* so that we can *plan* new *directions.*

Saturn, the ruling planet of Capricorn, offers *responsibility, discipline,* and *efficiency* in how we *manage* our *purpose* in *achieving* and *accomplishing* our *ambitions.*

Mars, the planet of action and doing is exalted in Capricorn. We can be most *effective* to *accomplish* our *work* when the actions of our *ambitions* are *integrated* and *organized* around right timing.

AQUARIUS

The fixed air sign of Aquarius is associated with our *community* of *friends, allies, groups,* and *societies.* They include not only those in close proximity, but also the *global community.* Aquarius includes being *humanitarian* for the well being of all planetary *communities* (*altruism*), including *social causes.* The sign has more to do with *groups* and *societies* than the individual.

Do your *friends* and *groups* enhance the Aquarian qualities of *freedom* and *independence* in you, or diminish those qualities through your *bondage* to those people? Aquarian energy can also *liberate* you from being in *bondage* to outmoded Capricorn restrictions and conservatism, giving you a new sense of *freedom* and *independence.*

Computers are included in Aquarius's domain. They allow the *global mind* to be connected via the *Internet.*

Aquarian energy can be *unconventional* when a *society* requires *reform. Revolutions* can be *rebellions* against *tyranny* to *liberate* people from *bondage.* The liabilities of Aquarius include allowing *mob* or *group consciousness* to dictate *social reform.* (The French *Revolution* is one glaring example of this.) Also, be *aware* of the tendency toward being *eccentric* (off center) or going to *extremes* just to be "*different.*" Consider being centered on the *awareness* of your uniqueness within the Infinite Mind.

Aquarius is the compliant sign for the Sun. If we are compliant to the Sun's light, we can shine in being *uniquely* who we are without going to the *extremes* of *rebellion* and being *eccentric.*

Aquarius is the receptive sign for Pluto. Authentic power avoids keeping others in *bondage* through *tyranny* or *mob rule.* Authentic power allows others the *freedom* and *independence* to live in an *altruistic society* of *differences.*

Saturn, one of two ruling planets for Aquarius, states that responsibility and *freedom* are interconnected. With responsibility *freedom* can be a *goal* for *friends, groups,* and *society,* and with *freedom* comes responsibility.

Uranus, the second ruling planet of Aquarius, offers change, awakening, and insight to the *humanitarian goals* of *friends, groups,* and *society.*

Aquarius is the exalted sign for Mercury. Mercury includes being *spontaneous* and *innovative by* being *aware* in the moment of unexpected connections with unusual and *extraordinary* people and situations. You can make the *extraordinary* the ordinary in your life.

PISCES

We are finishing up with the Piscean Age and entering the Aquarian Age. Piscean liabilities are explained in more detail here, since it is necessary for us to *release* these liabilities in order to enter the awareness of the

Aquarian Age.

In the mutable dual water sign of Pisces the *unconscious* has two parts—a higher part (*heaven*) and a lower part (*hell*). The lower *unconscious*—our *hellish* history—only repeats itself when we do not or will not revise or *release* it. The lower *unconscious* holds our *delusions* and *denials*. We must *release* (thereby *transcending*) the impressions of being a *victim, martyr, savior*, and *rescuer* to enter the Aquarian Age of Liberation and Awakening.

In Pisces you deal with issues of *trust*. Do you suspend your rational logical mind to *trust* your *intuitions* and Divine Guidance of the higher *unconscious*? All of us have had experiences in which we allowed our rational mind to override our *intuitions* because its message did not make rational sense to our conscious mind, only to discover later that our *intuitions* held accurate and *trustworthy* information.

Once I was getting ready to turn onto a freeway entrance ramp when I "heard" my *inner voice* suggest taking the arterial street. I *trusted* my rational mind that said, "Take the freeway—it will save time." Almost as soon as I got on the freeway, I saw that all the cars were jammed up and hardly moving!

At one time or another, most of us have exhibited misplaced *compassion* by playing *rescuer*. The scenario goes like this:

"Oh, here, let me help you."

"Who asked you for help?"

"Oh. You're right. You didn't ask me. I'll just mind my own business like I should have."

Acting from *real compassion* involves looking over a situation with clarity. If you are going to throw a lifeline from your boat to someone in the water, you should look for willingness to be *saved*! If the drowning person is trying to pull you into the water while you are trying to pull them out of the water (the *alcoholic* who says they will quit), what is *skewed* about that *picture*? They really do not want to do anything about *releasing* the *suffering* of their *predicament*.

Victim is defined here not as someone who is *victimized* by a *perpetrator*, but someone who has not made a reasonable effort in a reasonable amount of time to *release* their *victimization*. A *victim* then becomes a self-proclaimed *martyr*. Such a *victim* plays on other people's *compassion* and *empathy* with their *woe-is-me* story of what happened five years ago, as if it happened yesterday. Like a *psychic parasite*, they use their repetitious story to suck *compassion* and *sympathy* from others.

How can you tell if you are in the presence of such a person? After they have told you their story for the umpteenth time, they say, "Oh, I feel so much better now." How do you feel? Drained, like your energy has just been sucked out of you. It has. Is it *compassion* to let someone drain your energy?

What are your *dreams*? Are they *inspired* with *imaginative vision* or the *mirage* of *delusional nightmares*? *Inspiring dreams* can be from the *fantasies* of our *daydreams* fueled by our imagination.

Our *projection* of both irrational *fear (paranoia)* and *guilt* (*victimizing* by *blaming* ourselves or others as *scapegoats*) causes *suffering*. What we *project* out of our lower *unconscious* (disowning the *fear* or *guilt*) is where we *crucify* ourselves through *betraying* and *victimizing* ourselves. The alternative is *believing* the *dreams* of our inspirations as Divine Guidance.

We periodically experience our "*escape* clause" in Pisces, the sign of the dual *fish*. Are we *escaping reality* by sinking deeper into our lower *unconscious* on a downward spiral? The three D's of *deception, denial*, and *delusion* is how we continue to *victimize* ourselves with our irrational *fears* and *guilt*. Or do we surface with the clarity of Vision and inspiration in an upward spiral into *reality*? We then *transcend* the *suffering* caused by our *deceptions, denials* and *delusions*. The healing and *releasing* of our past allows us to have an *inspired* vision of the future. The difference is *hell* or *heaven*.

Pisces is the compliant sign of Mercury. By being conscious of *Reality*, we can *release, escape*, and *transcend projecting* outside of ourselves our *irrational fears* and the *guilt*. They *victimize* us with the three D's of *deception, denial*, and *delusion*.

Jupiter, one of two ruling planets for Pisces, offers its *mercy* and *compassion* to help others who are not as *fortunate* as we are.

Neptune, the second ruling planet for Pisces, offers the intuition of our inner senses (inner sight, hearing, and sensing) as Inner Guidance for our *faith, trust*, and *dreams*.

Venus, the planet of love and peace, is exalted in Pisces. We are Piscean *Blessing Angels* when we send out *universal love* through *prayer*, especially to those who are *suffering* and in need of *faith*.

The following key word phrases will assist you in remembering the qualities of the signs:

Aries: I lead
Taurus: I value
Gemini: I know
Cancer: I care
Leo: I love
Virgo: I serve
Libra: I decide
Scorpio: I empower
Sagittarius: I aspire
Capricorn: I achieve
Aquarius: I befriend
Pisces: I envision

The following synopsis recaps the assets and liabilities of each sign:

Sign	**Assets**	**Liabilities**
Aries	courage, strength	selfishness, hatred
Taurus	stewardship, self-esteem	stingy, uneconomical
Gemini	intelligent, knowledge	inconsistent, superficial
Cancer	caring, protective	moody, neglectful
Leo	generous, creative	arrogant, melodramatic
Virgo	service, discerning	judgmental, unhealthy
Libra	peaceful, considerate	procrastination, unfair
Scorpio	passion, empowered	grievances, manipulative
Sagittarius	open-minded, enthusiastic	self-righteous, intolerant
Capricorn	ambitious, patience	pessimistic, irresponsible
Aquarius	humanitarian, independent	eccentric, extreme
Pisces	compassion, intuitive	unrealistic, denial

Your Rising Sign (Ascendant)

In your natal chart the 9 o'clock position is at the eastern point of the circle where the sky meets the earth. It shows what is called your Rising Sign or Ascendant. Your Rising Sign shows your self-image—how you see yourself. It also influences your body type and appearance. You assert who you are through the qualities of your Rising Sign.

At the western point of the circle, 180 degrees opposite your Ascendant, at the 3 o'clock position of the circle, is your Descendant. At this position above this horizontal line on the page of "Planetary Motions" is the sign of Libra. The glyph for Libra looks like a setting Sun with the straight line for the horizon underneath it.

Every action in Aries has an opposite and equal reaction in Libra, the opposite sign. The polarity of Aries and Libra is cause and effect, reaping what you sow, action and reaction.

Remember the saying "as within so without." The action, cause, and sowing begins at the 9 o'clock point called the Ascendant or Rising Sign and the effect, reaction, and reaping comes back to you at the 3 o'clock point, called the Descendant.

The Aquarian Age

Every Age lasts about 2100 years. We are moving out of the Piscean Age into the Aquarian Age. The Aquarian Age is all about the awakening process. One of the emphases for Aquarius is awakening to the sisterhood and brotherhood of humanity. If the polar wobble of the earth is altered by the ice caps melting, reducing the massive weight at the poles, or by some other factor, the Aquarian Age might arrive sooner than anticipated. The sacred writings of the ancients might be describing this change happening in "a twinkling of an eye." The home planet of Aquarius is Uranus, which includes the qualities of sudden, unexpected change.

When astrologers talk about the natural order of the constellations they go from Aquarius to Pisces. The Ages progress in reverse order, backwards to the natural order, repeating about every 26,000 years. This order has to do with what is called the precession of the equinoxes caused by the Earth's wobble on its axis, like a top trying to right itself. This circle is a different time line than the natural zodiac of astrology. Basically the degree of the spring and autumn equinoxes changes by one degree every 72 years as measured against the backdrop of the constellations of astronomy, not the zodiac of astrology.

Scientists have found tropical fossils at the poles and glacial silt at the equator. Could this phenomena be from the poles reversing their positive and negative polarity? The Earth's tone as a frequency has been dramatically shifting as the magnetic polarity between the poles gets ready to reverse the positive and negative charge at each pole. The Earth does not flip its axis, only the polarity between its poles. Gregg Braden discusses this phenomenon of polar magnetic shifts in his writings.

One theory is that the duality of energies on Earth is being amplified, as time seems to be speeding up. We are experiencing a wake-up call from the Divine. Rather than "many are called and few are chosen," everyone is being called. We each have a decision to answer that call and wake up or not.

Chapter 5 discusses the houses—the sections of "pie"—dividing the circle of the zodiac.

Chapter 5

HOUSES

Planets are the generators of the energy of what is going on in your life. The signs are how the planets' energy can be expressed. Houses represent where the action of the planets is playing out. The circle representing the zodiac is divided into twelve segments or "houses" like pieces of pie or spokes of a wheel. The wheel spokes are called cusps. The line between Aries and Pisces at 9 o' clock represents the cusp for the first house. The area of the first house is represented by the space between this cusp and the next counter-clockwise cusp. The houses have a similar meaning as the signs in their natural counter-clockwise order around the wheel, beginning with Aries energy representing the first house. The sign at the end of each cusp that rules and influences that house in your natal chart is rarely the same as the natural sign associated with that house. The sign that rules and thereby influences each house is on the cusp of that house.

The point at 9 o'clock on the horizontal line of your natal chart is called the Rising Sign, which rules your first house. The Rising Sign has a first house interpretation for everyone. The sign on the first house cusp as your Rising Sign colors and influences your first house self-image and appearance. Refer to the "Signs of the Zodiac" and "Moon Through the Signs" sections to learn the influence of each sign as a Rising Sign.

You can use the houses to locate the houses of the New and Full Moon cycles in your natal chart if you are living in the same time zone and hemisphere of your birth. Otherwise, you will need to have a relocation chart done which shows the electromagnetic shift your biology has gone through by moving to a different time zone. (Jet lag is partially caused by this electromagnetic shift of flying across different time zones.)

You can see in the *Celestial Guide®* that the degrees of the New and Full Moons are given to the left of the sign and the minutes to the right of the sign on the day of their occurrence. Round off to the nearest degree by rounding down if the minutes are from 1 to 29. Round up if the minutes are from 30 to 59. For example, if the Moon is at 22°18', round off to 22°. If the Moon is at 22°33', round off to 23°. Once you have the nearest degree of the New or Full Moon sign, you can pinpoint the house placement in your chart and interpret not only the sign meaning but also the house meaning each month for the New and Full Moons.

You can plot the place of the New Moon by what house the sign and degree of the New Moon falls. You can do the same for each Full Moon. Find the sign on the house cusp of your natal chart that matches the sign of the New or Full Moon. The degree of the New or Full Moon will be on either side of this cusp. If that degree is greater than the degree on the house cusp, the New or Full Moon will be in the house counter-clockwise from the cusp. If the degree is less than the degree on the house cusp the New or Full Moon will be in the house clockwise from the cusp.

The houses also have traditional meanings of detriment or fall for all planets traveling through them. The same application of compliant and receptive meanings for the signs can also be applied to the houses. If the New or Full Moon occurs in your second house then you read the meaning of the sign Taurus for the second house. If the New or Full Moon occurs in your tenth house then you read the meaning of the sign Capricorn for the tenth house. Every month you can track the influence of the New and Full Moon in your chart by this simple method. You will know the influence of both the New and Full Moons by the signs that they occur in as well as in what house they occur specifically to your chart. The next chapter will explain how you can add the meaning of the planetary alignments called aspects to the sign and house placement of the New and Full Moons.

Chapter 6

ASPECTS

Following the section in the *Celestial Guide*® describing the qualities of the planets is a section called "Aspects." Aspects are the geometric angles that the planets form with each other. Review this section, noting the symbols for the five aspects: conjunction, sextile, square, trine, and opposition. Aspects are given in the lower right-hand corner of each day's date. They are listed for almost every day in the *Celestial Guide*®; only occasionally will there be a day with no aspects. Almost all aspects are from the Moon. However, occasionally you will see a planet other than the Moon making an aspect to another planet.

Aspects are divided into two categories: harmonic and discordant. The traditional label for harmonic aspects is easy or favorable. I prefer to call harmonic aspects "grace" aspects. By that I mean that the aspect can be your grace because you have put out harmonious energy for it to return to you as an event of grace. Grace aspects represent harmonic flows of positive karma, opportunities, and open doors. Knowing "grace" aspects from current planetary positions to planets in your chart can help you recognize and make the most out of opportunities presented to you.

Sextiles and trines are grace aspects. Conjunctions are mostly grace, depending on the planets involved and what sign they are in. For instance, Mars conjunct Venus could be the grace of a marriage proposal, however, you may not accept the offer. During a conjunction the planets are in the same place in the zodiac. Their energies blend like ingredients in a recipe.

Oppositions can be grace, again depending on the planets involved and what sign they are in. Mars opposite Venus could be fireworks and a really great time for a couple, or it may be discordant energy between them.

Using archaic terms for discordant aspects such as "hard," "difficult," or "unfavorable" perpetuates an unnecessarily negative perception. I prefer the term "mastery" aspects, which manifest as challenges, potential healings, or lessons to be mastered. A mastery aspect infers an empowering learning process that, when completed, de-magnetizes us from attracting further experiences regarding that particular lesson. Just because we have a natal, transiting, or progressed square doesn't necessarily mean something "unsettling" has to come up if we have cleared the pattern. The strongest mastery aspect is a square, which is a 90° angle between two planets. The next strongest mastery angle is the opposition (180° angle), followed by the conjunction, depending on the nature of the planets involved and what sign they are in. Oppositions are usually experienced as a mastery until you master them, depending on the planets involved and what sign they are in.

Once you have mastered that potential discordant energy, you have cleared the pattern. No resonance or vibrational pattern exists within you to attract the dissonant pattern into your life again, even when a transiting planet forms a mastery angle to a planet in your natal chart.

It can be beneficial to schedule a counseling or therapy session based on a mastery day in your chart cycles. If you have not had an issue triggered before your session, the issue can be easily accessed during the session and more easily cleared.

Some astrology books suggest that if you have a square aspect, you had better stay home because it could be one of the worst days of your life. Not necessarily so. If you have cleared the pattern, then you have mastered it; it will not come up in your life. What often happens at those mastery times is that you attract another into your life who is going through a similar process to one that you have mastered. You have healed the issue; you have cleared it. You now have the wisdom of that experience to pass on to the other person. They have the choice of listening to good advice from someone who has been there and done that or to learn in their own way, which is usually harder and more difficult.

Unfortunately, too many astrology books imply that the dynamics of the mastery aspects are set throughout your whole life; that you are going to have a whole lifetime of being in a certain difficult condition, such as being poor or not finding a compatible mate. No, you cannot grow a leg back, but you can change your energy patterns. There are some fatalistic teachings out there, so please use discernment when reading astrology books.

Remember that oppositions are both grace and mastery. They act as either complementary or conflicting mirrors of the energetic imprint you have with specific planets at a particular time in your life. The conflicting mirror acts as if another is opposing you, or reflects something in your nature that requires healing and correction, but which you have disclaimed as an issue. Another interpretation is that you may be required to stand up with your skills and strength to the issue presented. The complementary opposition will act as an attractor field of at least one opportunity, or of someone giving you complimentary feedback about the qualities they admire or appreciate in you.

Find the "Aspects of the Moon" section. It lists the different geometric angles that the Moon makes to the other planets in its 28-day revolution around the Earth, and the influences of the Moon as it aspects the various planets. The last listing explains the Moon aspecting the Sun in each of the Moon's phases. Each of these aspects between the Sun and Moon happens every month.

In the upper right hand corner of a date with the darkened face of a New Moon and a date with the lit face of the Full Moon, the sign and time that the Moon aspects the Sun are listed. Below this marking, in the lower right hand corner of the day where the aspects are always listed, the time of the conjunction or opposition is repeated. In the upper right hand corner of the day for a Quarter Moon, the sign and time of the aspect are listed. Below this marking, in the lower right hand corner of the day where aspects are listed, the square between the Moon and Sun as an aspect is listed, followed by the time of the Quarter Moon.

A conjunction between the Sun and Moon means that they are in the same place in the sky, which happens once every 30 days. The New Moon day is the only day we cannot see the Moon as the whole dark side faces the Earth.

When the Sun is setting in the west the Full Moon is rising in the east. They are always opposite each other on the Full Moon. On those days the Full Moon is always shown in opposition (180°) to the Sun as an aspect.

The Quarter Moons are always square the Sun. A square is literally a square, a 90° right angle. Looking at the zodiac wheel, a square would be between a planet at 9 o'clock and one at either 12 or 6 o'clock. A square can also be depicted by a planet at 3 o'clock and one at either 12 or 6 o'clock. The First Quarter Moon is always straight south 90° from the setting Sun. The Last Quarter Moon is always straight south 90° from the rising Sun. A square is the most challenging aspect because it causes a stressful friction of energy between the two planets. When alternating electric current is in a square sine wave, it is said to be out of phase. This is similar to what is happening with a square aspect.

Remember that the beginning time of every Void of Course period is listed in the upper right hand corner of the date. You will also see the Moon aspecting a planet at the same time in the lower right hand corner of that day. At the time the Moon goes Void of Course you will always see an aspect listed between the Moon and another planet.

The planets produce resonances that influence you. Remember the example of two guitars side by side having the same tunings? Plucking a string on one guitar will resonate as the same tone on the other guitar string of the same tuning. Resonances also occur between you and the planets. An aspect in your natal chart can resonate with the same transiting planetary aspect, manifesting as an event in your experience. In other words, if you have the same planetary aspect in your chart as what is in the *Celestial Guide®* on a given date, you will more likely experience an event or psychological state associated with that aspect.

For instance, if you have the Moon trine Uranus in your chart, note in the *Celestial Guide®* twice a month the day when the Moon trines Uranus. See if anything happens on that day related to the aspect. If you have Venus square Neptune in your chart, note any day that you see Venus square Neptune.

A general rule for the timing of events associated with aspects between planets in the *Celestial Guide®*, especially ones that duplicate aspects in your natal chart, is as follows: For the Moon aspecting a planet, allow about 12 hours before to about 6 hours after the aspect for an event to take place. (This period of influence is called an orb.) For instance, if the aspect says 4:00 PM, the event could show up as early as 4:00 AM or as late as 10:00 PM. The exceptions to this rule are aspects to Pluto, aspects from the Moon in Scorpio, and aspects to planets in Scorpio, which tend to be delayed more than other aspects. The rule is reversed in these cases. Allow about 6 hours before to about 12 hours after the exact time listed for these aspects. For instance, if the Moon aspect is 11:00 AM, the event could show up as early as 5:00 AM or as late as 11:00 PM.

For an aspect from the Sun, Mercury, or Venus to any planet, allow approximately 24 hours before and after the exact aspect in the *Celestial Guide®* for a possible event to happen. For an aspect from Mars, allow +

or −3 days from the day of the aspect. An aspect from Jupiter gets + or −5 days from the day of the aspect. An aspect from Saturn gets + or −7 days from the day of the aspect. The invisible planets have a much greater time of potential influence since they move more slowly. An aspect from Uranus gets + or −20 days from the day of the aspect. An aspect from either Neptune gets + or −25 days and Pluto gets + or −30 days from the day of the aspect.

When the Moon conjuncts one of the visible planets you can view them near each other in the night sky around the time listed for the conjunction. The Moon and Venus are particularly beautiful when they are conjunct after sunset or before sunrise. If you view the Moon a day before, the day of, and a day after a conjunction with a visible planet like Venus, you will see how much the Moon moves around the Earth in a day—about 12°. Multiply the distance you observe by 28 and you can understand how the Moon travels a full circle around the Earth in that time. If you see the eclipse indication as a darkened circle for the Moon conjuncting a planet, they will be very, very close to each other. If you are in the right location on the Earth, the Moon will actually pass in front of the planet, eclipsing it from right to left.

To get a barometer of the astrological weather for any particular day in the *Celestial Guide*®, give each aspect listed on a particular day a (+) or (−) using the following code: a conjunction gets both a (+) and (−), a square gets a (−), a sextile and trine each get a (+), and an opposition also gets both a (+) and (−). Then add up the pluses and minuses for that particular day. For example, if a day has a conjunction (+ and −), a square (−), and a trine (+), your score for the day would be 2 pluses and 2 minuses.

You can get a general overview for the day by reading the description of the Moon sign (include the sign's element) on that day. Notice if the day has only grace aspects, only mastery aspects, or a combination of grace and mastery aspects like the two pluses and two minuses in the above example. You would look for an emphasis of the assets or liabilities, or both possibilities of that sign, depending on the aspect score for the day. If a day had only grace aspects you would expect the day to go smoothly. If the day had only mastery aspects you or someone you know would expect to potentially have at least one difficulty, issue, or healing arise during the day.

The aspect symbols in your natal chart can be easily given a score by using the following method. List each of your planets in a descending order somewhere on your natal chart. After each planet, place a plus or a minus for each grace or mastery aspect listed in the aspect section of your natal chart. Give each planet a plus for conjunctions, sextiles, trines, and oppositions. Give each planet a minus for conjunctions, squares, and oppositions. Then add up the pluses and minuses for the total score for each planet. You now have a summary of each of your planet's overall grace and mastery aspects, similar to scoring the day's aspects in the *Celestial Guide®*.

For example, if Venus in your natal chart has aspects to other planets of a sextile (+), trine (+), and opposition (+ and –), the score for your Venus would be three pluses and one minus. You can then interpret that your Venus has potentially more grace than mastery for your life. You would give more weight to the grace qualities of whatever sign Venus is in than to the mastery qualities.

What if the reverse were true for a planet? What if the planet had more mastery aspects to other planets than grace? If your natal Sun had a conjunction (+ and –) and a square (–) for a score of 1 plus and 2 minuses, you would focus more on the mastery-sounding traits of whatever sign the planet is in. These traits indicate that you have some work to do to correct potential problems with that planet's expression in whatever sign it occupies in your natal chart.

When you have a transit or progression to any natal planet you can evaluate the potential strength of the cycle by checking the score for the planet being activated in your natal chart. A grace cycle to the natal planet will be stronger, the higher your grace score is to that planet. A mastery cycle to the natal planet will be stronger, the higher your mastery score is to that planet.

Also note if the transiting planet is already connected by natal aspect to a natal planet. If it is in a natal grace aspect to another planet, then grace cycles from either planet to the other will be stronger than if they were not aspected at birth. For example, if Mars sextiles Mercury natally, then grace aspects from transiting Mercury to Mars or transiting Mars to Mercury will be stronger than usual.

Similarly if a transiting planet is in a natal mastery aspect then mastery cycles from either planet to the other will be stronger than if they were not aspected at birth. For example if Mars squares Mercury natally, then mastery transits of Mercury to Mars or Mars to Mercury will be stronger.

Furthermore, if you have two planets in grace aspect natally, whenever they form mastery aspects in your cycles they will not be as strong as usual. For example, you have the Sun trine Jupiter in your natal chart. Whenever the transiting Sun squares natal Jupiter, or transiting Jupiter squares natal Sun, the mastery aspect will not be as strong as usual.

Conversely, if you have two planets in mastery aspect natally, then when they form grace aspects in your cycles, they will not be as strong as usual. For example, the Sun squares Jupiter in your natal chart. Whenever the transiting Sun trines natal Jupiter or transiting Jupiter trines natal Sun the grace aspect will not be as strong as usual.

The planets in fixed signs have the strongest ingrained grace and mastery aspects, followed by planets in cardinal signs, followed by planets in mutable signs.

Whenever you have an aspect from the New or Full Moons to any planet in your chart, you can use the key word lists in Chapters 9 and 10 to better understand that planet's influence for the particular lunar cycle. If the New or Full Moon activates your Mars in Taurus, then read about Mars on the planet key word list and Taurus on the sign key word list to discover which qualities could be activated into your life.

Emphasize the grace or mastery traits, depending on what aspect the New or Full Moon makes to your Mars. If the alignment is grace, then pick out the grace words of Mars in Taurus to be emphasized during the lunar cycle. If the alignment is mastery, then pick out the mastery words of Mars in Taurus to be emphasized during the lunar cycle. They will help you key into how your life experiences relate and connect to Mars in Taurus for that particular Lunar cycle.

The three primary aspects to pay attention to every New and Full Moon are their conjunctions, squares, and oppositions to other planets in your natal chart. I allow a plus or minus 3° influence from the nearest degree of the New and Full Moons for any planetary aspects in my natal chart. A conjunction would be within 3° of the exact rounded off degree of the New and Full Moons. For instance, if the New Moon is at 10° in Libra, then the influence extends from 7° to 13° Libra as a conjunction. If you have Venus at 8° Libra in your natal chart, then the New Moon at 10° will be conjunct your 8° Venus, since it is 2° away from the New Moon.

The same degree spread of influence will apply to all major aspects from this Libra point in your natal chart. The square is four signs in each direction counting the sign of the New or Full Moon as one. Think of the square as a four-sided figure. You find the exact square at the same degree of the New or Full Moon plus or minus 3° in the squared sign. In this instance the square would be four signs in either direction along the zodiac from Libra, which would be backward four signs to Cancer and forward four signs to Capricorn. Count them on the circle of your natal chart or the "Planetary Motion" chart.

An opposition is the opposite sign from the New or Full Moon. Again use the same degree as the New or Full Moon. Count 3° in both directions in the opposite sign using the exact degree of the New or Full Moon. For instance, for the New Moon in Libra at 10°, the influence extends to any planet from 7° to 13° in the opposite sign of Aries.

If the New or Full Moon is conjunct within 3° of the degree of your Sun, Moon, or Rising Sign, then you will be more strongly influenced by the sign's energy than if you just had the New or Full Moon in the signs. If the New or Full Moon aspect is within 3° of a planet or Rising Sign in your natal chart, then its influence will be more strongly activated for four weeks for the New Moon or two weeks for the Full Moon.

In the "Aspects" section you can look up the meaning of the Moon aspecting any planet. For instance, if the New Moon is conjunct your Venus, you can look up Moon conjunct Venus and have an idea of what will be emphasized in your life for the four-week New Moon cycle. If the Full Moon is opposite your Saturn, then you can look up Moon opposite Saturn and have an idea of what will be emphasized in your life for the two-week Full Moon cycle.

In the following two chapters, I suggest meditations for the New and Full Moons.

Enjoy celestial navigating!

Chapter 7

NEW MOON MEDITATIONS

The following New Moon meditations are most effective when done at least once a day in the morning for 28 days from the day of the New Moon. The key words of the signs are in italics. You may want to write the statement and then repeat it like a mantra up to three times as you meditate or contemplate its meaning. Saying and writing the key words aligns you to seeding the qualities of that sign for the four-week cycle of the New Moon's influence. The statements are deliberately written with "I am..." because those words have maximum power to manifest what you are affirming. The present tense is used because the now is your only time of empowerment. These statements can also be used for a planet in a particular sign when it is activated by transits and progressions.

Aries

I am *courageously asserting* myself with an infusion of *life force energy*.

I am *motivated* to *initiate* new *actions* as the *leader* of my life.

Taurus

I am *valuing* and *appreciating* all that I have *attained* and all that I have been *given* in being a *steward* of Earth's *resources.*

I am *utilizing* my *talents, gifts*, and *potential* to the best of my *ability*.

Gemini

I am clearly *perceiving* and correctly *interpreting* whatever I give my *attention* to.

I am seeking new *interests* to stimulate my *curiosity* and *learning*.

Cancer

I am *nurturing* others and myself with *caring* and *preserving* those things that *support life*.

I am *providing comfort, support*, and *security* to my *family*, including my "extended" *family*.

Leo

I am *love, co-creating* with my *Divine Will.*

I am *loving* all *children* as well as involving my *Inner Child* in *recreation* and *entertainment.*

Virgo

I am being an objective *witness/observer* with right *discernment* that includes the relevant *details* of living.

I am *cleansing* and *purifying* my body and mind as a *sacred* space and place for my *mental* and *physical health.*

Libra

I am making *decisions* based on the highest good for all involved.

I am promoting *peace* and *mutual cooperation, consideration*, and *thoughtfulness.*

Scorpio

I am *empowering* myself to *transmute* all *grievances* into *forgiveness.*

I am feeling the *intensity* of my *passion* as my *power* to *manifest* my *desire(s)* to [name your desire(s)].

Sagittarius

I am *expanding* my *horizons* by *broadening* my *mind* with new *adventures.*

I am *fueling* my *aspirations* and *intentions* with *enthusiasm* and *optimism.*

Capricorn

I am *managing* my life with *practical planning, organization*, and *responsibility.*

I am *successfully achieving* my *purpos*e with *integrity* and right *timing.*

Aquarius

I am being *innovative* in my life with *originality* and *spontaneity* to think outside the "box."

I am *awakening* to my *awareness* of *liberating* the *human spirit* within me for all *humanity.*

Pisces

I am *trusting* the overview and *intuitions* of my *Inner Guidance.*

I am *inspired* with *blessings* and *grace* to live the *reality* of *miracle-mindedness.*

(Any extension of *boundless* love that *releases* others from their *suffering* is a *miracle.*)

Chapter 8

FULL MOON MEDITATIONS

For maximum effectiveness, I recommend doing the following Full Moon meditations at least once a day in the morning for 12 days from the Full Moon day. These meditations are written with the key words of the signs in italics. The key words for the sign of the Full Moon are given toward the beginning of the statements. The key words for the sign of the Sun being opposite the Full Moon are given toward the end of the statements. You may want to write the statement and then repeat it up to three times like a mantra as you meditate or contemplate its meaning. Saying and writing the key words aligns you to the qualities of that sign for the two-week cycle of the Full Moon's influence. The statements are deliberately written with "I am..." because those words have maximum power to manifest what you are affirming. The present tense is used because the now is your only time of empowerment. These statements can also be used for a planet in a particular sign when it is opposed by a transiting planet or progressed Moon.

Aries-Libra

I am *asserting* that my *strength* and *vitality* add to the *mutual accord* with others and the *decisions* that involve them.

I am *acting* towards others as I would like to be *treated*.

Taurus-Scorpio

I am *giving* to others and *receiving* from others in *mutual abundance* and *prosperity*.

I am increasing my *self-esteem* by *investing* in experiences that *empower* me.

Gemini-Sagittarius

I am *learning* with *understanding* and *wisdom*.

I am having a *mental outlook* that is *enthusiastic* and *optimistic*.

Cancer-Capricorn

I am *caring* for myself and others with appropriate *boundaries.*

I am *supporting* my *lifestyle* with *purposeful work* that *honors* the *accomplishments* of others.

Leo-Aquarius

I am maintaining my *individuality* within all *friendships, groups,* and *social organizations.*

I am *expressing* myself with regard for the *independence* and *freedom* of others.

Virgo-Pisces

I am *serving* others with *realistic compassion.*

I am *devoted* to *healing suffering, delusions,* and *denials* into the *reality* of *universal love.*

Libra-Aries

I am *complimenting* and *appreciating* the *courage* and *leadership* of others.

I am *committed* to *fairness* and *equal rights* as a *peaceful warrior.*

Scorpio-Taurus

I am *desiring* to *empower* others with a sense of their *self-worth.*

I am making *financial investments* that enhance the *beauty* and *preciousness* of Earth's *resources.*

Sagittarius-Gemini

I am *wisely* infusing the *arrow* of my *intentions* with *consistent attention.*

I am *open-minded* to *expanding* my *truths* of life by *learning* new *information.*

Capricorn-Cancer

I am *disciplined* in my *time* to *manage* my *career/profession* and *home/family.*

I am *responsible* in my *purpose* to *preserve* and *care* for the *ecology* that *supports* all life.

Aquarius-Leo

I am *aware* of *Infinite Mind* blended with *Divine Love* in my life.

I am aligned with the *innovation* and *originality* of my *heart's creativity.*

Pisces-Virgo

I am a *blessing angel* of Light to all that I *witness.* (Send Light to any situation you observe that is not peaceful. The word "angel" originally meant "messenger" or "intermediary.")

I am having a *realistic* balance between my *intuitions* and *ideals,* and *discerning* mind.

Chapter 9

PLANETARY KEYWORDS

Planets only generate positive constructive energy. Their energy generated through the signs has positive and negative meanings because human choices and behavior determines how a planet's energy is expressed in the signs. The misapplication of a planet's energy is the result of human dysfunction and distortion of its energy, which is why negative traits are part of a sign's description and not part of a planet's description.

Sun

Light, Spirit, Source, Self, life force, illumination, enlightenment, Love, Will, create, authority, center

Moon

Mother, women, body, fertility, nurture, nourish, instincts, feelings, moods, receptive, personality, the masses

Mercury

Conscious mind, communication, perception, thoughts, senses, messages, mobility, flexibility, adaptability, youthful

Venus

Feminine, female, yin, social and material values, quality, aesthetics, harmony, peace, beauty, romance, attraction, affection, artists,

Mars

Masculine, male, men, yang, physical energy, action, force, motivate, initiate, assert, fire

Jupiter

Supraconscious, Truth, archetypes, symbols, benevolence, optimism, abundance, increase, magnify, expand

Saturn

Structure, design, pattern, timing, coincidence, synchronicity, concentration, limits, father, older people

Uranus

Infinite Mind, change, unexpected, sudden, awaken, liberate, original, unorthodox, insight, telepathy, unusual, unique, revolutionary, nonconformity, astrology

Neptune

Unconscious, inner senses, vision, Divine Guidance, projection, imagination, impressions, clarity, inspiration, ocean

Pluto

Subconscious, power, catharsis, metamorphosis, transformation, regeneration, renewal, transmute, birth, emerge, death, decay, rebirth, hidden, eliminate, recycle

North Node

Future growth, potential abilities, development, exertion.

South Node

Habits, motives, inertia, past efforts and developed qualities.

Chapter 10

SIGN KEYWORDS

The signs have both positive and negative meanings because human choices and behavior determine how a planet's energy is expressed in the signs. The misapplication of a planet's energy is the result of human dysfunction and distortion of that energy, which is why negative traits are part of a sign's description.

A planet in a sign emphasizes that sign's assets (strengths) and liabilities (weaknesses) more than those signs in which you have no planets. The more planets you have in a sign the more its traits will be emphasized in your life.

The part of the body that is related to each sign is listed at the end of each sign's traits

ARIES

Self-image, character traits, body type and appearance, strength, assertive, initiative, motivation, confidence, (dis)courage, encourage, motivation, impulse, effort, be, doing, actions, resilience, selfish, willful, aggressive, competitive, impatient, dominate, argumentative, resistance, inhibit, macho, hate, attack, weapons, mechanical objects, warrior, pioneer, leader; head.

TAURUS

Material values and priorities, self-worth, self-esteem, beauty of form, talents, gifts, abilities, cultivate, build, possessions, resources, finances, accounting, ownership, acquire, receiving and giving, stewardship, goods, products, (un)economical, frugal, conserve, stingy, poverty, greed, endurance, perseverance, stubbornness, productive, usefulness, farmer, builder, economist; throat.

GEMINI

Knowledge, intelligent, K-12 education, learn, words, writing, story, humor, attention, information, idea, belief, attitude, opinion, interpret, conclusion, comprehension, true/false, (in)correct, (dis)honest, reason, logic, memory, curiosity, games, immediate environment, brothers and sisters, neighbors, letters, phone calls, cities, short journeys, media, news, gossip, diversity, duality, inconsistent, interference, superficial, ignorance, stupidity, messenger, teacher, student, comedian; brain, arms, shoulders, lungs, nervous system.

CANCER

Maternal, domestic, home, family, care, (in)security, support, protection, safety, neglect, comfort, foundation, tradition, conventional, sentimental, moody, nation, roots, races, ancestors, nature, land, preservation, ecology, endings and beginnings, reject, abandon, mother, naturalist, historian; stomach, breasts.

LEO

Love, will, individuality (Self or ego), self-expression, (mis)create, loyalty, generous, (melo)drama, recreation, entertainment, loved ones, children, romantic involvements, fear, arrogance, pride, humiliation, performer, actor, inner child; heart, back.

VIRGO

Service, physical and mental health, heal, fix, self-help, hygiene, diet, purity, assimilation, analysis, evaluation, discernment, assessment, doubt, specifics, detail, criticism, judgment, condemnation, prejudice, bias, techniques, methods, devotion, tools, student-teacher/employer-employee, craftsmanship, skills, precision, apprenticeship, dedication, shy, modest, dexterity, pets, healer, instructor, apprentice, judge; hands and fingers, small intestines.

LIBRA

Social values, intimate and business partnerships, cooperate, balance, acceptance, approval, equality, (un)fair, commitment, harmony, peace, conflict, discord, choices, decisions, procrastination, agreements, compromise, double standards, counseling, negotiation, mediation, justice, manners, aesthetics, tact, thoughtful, considerate, appreciation, dependable, marketing, artist, romantic, counselor; kidneys.

SCORPIO

Subconscious, underworld, cocoon, use/misuse/abuse of power; empower, ritual, shamanic, manifest, desires, passion, constructive, destructive, defense, (in)vulnerable, control, manipulate, jealousy, revenge, grievance, secret, shadow, sabotage, forgiveness, joint power, sexuality, intense, surrender, investments, banking, debts, taxes, inheritance, insurance, waste, stagnant, detective, shaman, alchemist, mid-wife; large intestine, reproductive and eliminative organs.

SAGITTARIUS

Supraconscious, wisdom, symbols, signs, meaning, intention, affirm, open-minded, (mis)understanding, holistic, unity, principles, ethics, morals, human & divine laws, spirituality, metaphysics, religion, philosophy, psychology, college, aspiration, joy, enthusiasm, sports, outdoors, adventure, long journeys, destination, country, publishing, fanatic, self-righteous, dogmatic, hypocrisy, intolerant, high priestess/priest, traveler, professor, seeker; hips.

CAPRICORN

Paternal, (ir)responsible, discipline, organization, direction, plans, maps, boundaries, destiny, purpose, ambition, business, job, profession, work, achieve, accomplish, schedules, appointments, recognition, position, status, accountability, (dis)honor, reliable, integrity, impeccable, efficient, effective, time, patience, caution, delay, practical, management, government, rigid, pessimism, depression, disappointment, father, official, architect; bones, teeth, skin.

AQUARIUS

Goals, groups, ally, friends, community, society, clubs, mob, freedom, bondage, enslave, independence, rebellious, extreme, extraordinary, original, unconventional, innovative, spontaneous, radical, reform, aloof, (in)humane, philanthropy, altruism, electric, electronics, computers, internet, global mind, maverick, inventor, rebel, humanitarian; ankles, circulation.

PISCES

Unconscious, rectification of karma, (un)real, release, heaven, angels, transcendence, empathy, compassion, mercy, intuition, paranormal, (dis) appearance(s), ideals, trust, faith, miracles, believe, denial, deception, illusion, delusion, confusion, vague, (un)fortunate, suffering, irrational fear and guilt, escape, victim, betrayal, rescue, martyr, disassociation, hypnosis, project, scapegoat, isolation, loneliness, solitude, withdrawn, (in) sanity, confinement (hospitals, jails, prisons), hell, visual, image, dreams, nightmares, fantasy, focus, film, movies, television, video, visionary, rescuer, prophet; feet.

ABOUT THE AUTHOR

Anold Lane (pronounced a-NOLD) has been working in the healing arts for over 30 years. As a Revolutionary Astrologer, he has written for several magazines and newspapers and presented his craft on talk radio in several states. He has taught metaphysical classes and led numerous retreats.

While living in Hawaii, Anold was presented with an opportunity to combine his talent as a professional musician with his love for alternative healing through a technology known as the Sound Table. As a Sound Table practitioner, Anold has helped hundreds of people to dramatically improve the quality of their lives.

In addition, Anold has developed a unique system for awakening to the essence of who you are known as Evolutionary Dialogues™. This process dissolves the mirages of the ego and accelerates our awakening and wholeness.

Anold currently lives in the Seattle area where he enjoys a practice as a gifted astrologer and Sound Table practitioner.

Other books by Anold Lane:

Encodings of Light: A profound system to awaken and empower you (ISBN: 978-0-9817137-0-0, published November, 2008)

Voice from the Wilderness (ISBN: 978-0-9817137-2-4, published April, 2009)

The Zodiac Within You: How All 12 Signs Impact Your Life (ISBN: 978-0-9843883-8-7, published November, 2011)

Contact Anold at:
www.encodingsofLight.com
encodingsofLight@yahoo.com

CPSIA information can be obtained
at www.ICGtesting.com
Printed in the USA
FSOW01n0636111115
13187FS